MORAL AND LEGAL REASONING

MORAL AND LEGAL REASONING

Samuel Stoljar

First published 1980
in the U.K.
and all other parts of the world
excluding the U.S.A. by
THE MACMILLAN PRESS LTD
London and Basingstoke

First published in the U.S.A. 1980 by
HARPER & ROW PUBLISHERS INC.
BARNES & NOBLE IMPORT DIVISION

ᴡ 15125 [8.95 . 3.81

British Library Cataloguing in Publication Data

Stoljar, Samuel Jacob
  Moral and legal reasoning
    1. Law and ethics   2. Legal reasoning
    I. Title
    170   BJ55

MACMILLAN ISBN 0 333 27771 6

BARNES & NOBLE ISBN 0 06 496570 8
LCN 79−55525

Printed in Great Britain

for *Margaret Stoljar*

Contents

Preface

This book pursues a number of related themes in moral and legal philosophy, with two themes, however, more central than the others. One overall theme seeks to expose a basic closeness between moral and legal reasoning especially where such reasoning relates to the way we rationally judge our inter-personal grievances, that is, the way we rationally support or justify, distinguish or qualify, oppose or dismiss our mutual claims or complaints. Another major theme tries to establish that to argue rationally is not just to give reasons, but, more importantly, is to give reasons capable of concluding an argument, these being reasons which can also be said to be right or wrong not from a prudential but a distinctly moral point of view. Without a moral content, we shall concomitantly suggest, legal rules would be a fortuitous heap of imperatives without any internal purpose or direction, operating essentially *ad hoc*, while without a legal connection morality tends to err about its true centre of gravity as it misses out on what are socially the most significant situations, in particular those having to do with avoidable harm or injury, precisely the cases in which moral argument acquires its greatest rational strength instead of remaining, as it does in most other areas, merely 'open' or persuasive.

I wish to thank quite a few Canberra friends patient enough to listen to earlier versions of sections of this book; and I am especially grateful to two colleagues, one philosopher, one lawyer, who read the whole manuscript and offered helpful and encouraging comments.

Canberra, October 1979   SAMUEL STOLJAR

1 Reasons and Rules

PRACTICAL AND THEORETICAL REASONS

What we do, how we act or behave in our lives with regard to ourselves or to others, is on one level certainly determined by our felt needs and wants, as instinct drives us, as inclination bids us do; but on another level is, or can be, influenced by reason or rational reflection, as when we consider what we should do, or why, or when we think about our choices as choices or about our actions in the light of their objectives or effects. Without this capacity to reason about, and in this way to direct or guide, our actions, we would have no sense of what it means to act, to act for a purpose, nor of the evidence upon which we act, nor of rules or principles that distinguish between right and wrong actions; we would only have feelings and desires, doing our things not as self-conscious or self-starting individuals but as animals or plants do. Human action would be scarcely distinguishable from bodily move-ments, from such things as falling down or falling sick which are physical events but are not actions; for human actions, precisely because they are guided or guidable by reasons, also offer themselves to being judged as to how well or wisely we act, or how ill or foolishly.

Now the reasons so guiding our actions commonly form part of rules; indeed it is now easier to say why we have rules, or what they are for or about: rules tell us, very broadly, what to do, or how to act, in order to bring about certain objects or ends, either with regard to physical things, or with regard to ourselves, or with regard to other persons especially where our actions impinge on them beneficially or detrimentally.

Moreover, in guiding our actions, rules presuppose that as guidable human agents we are both free and rational: free because of our natural capacity to pursue and press differential aims, to act differently from others when we so decide; rational because the reasons incorporated in the rules provide at least some knowledge of what, for certain purposes, we simply *have* to do, the rules thus communicating a sort of necessity about certain actions, sometimes called practical necessity, yet without abrogating our residual freedom not to comply.

The practical reasons designed to guide actions need to be distinguished from theoretical reasons. The latter give us knowledge of the world irrespective of, sometimes even in spite of, human actions or aims, hence knowledge of what is anyhow the case, of what is possible or probable, whereas practical reasons only convey the knowledge we need to achieve our self-chosen ends by our own actions. Theoretically we may have good reason to say that in many, if not all, cases it rains whenever the sky clouds over darkly; to believe in the possibility of rain would here rest on good ('reasonable') evidence, being a valid inductive or probabilistic inference from previous facts and as such also a useful addition to our 'objective' or scientific knowledge of what usually, albeit not invariably, occurs. Practically, we may have good reason to think that taking an umbrella would be a prudent precaution if, though only if, we wish not to get wet. A practical reason is not intended to explain why rain comes when it does or anything else about scientific meteorology; a practical reason can thus by-pass theoretical or scientific explanations; it has only to be informative, but does not have to make things intelligible as well; we need no meteorological knowledge to understand that an umbrella may prove helpful in the rain.[1] A practical reason, moreover, must be kept distinct from a purely personal or subjective one. If asked why we do not want to get wet, we may give as our reason a dislike of personal discomfort; and if asked why we dislike this, we would, as Hume observed, very soon come to a point at which further reason-giving would have to stop, having reached a basic personal preference, that of wanting to avert unpleasantness or pain.[2]

If personal ends are eminently variable depending on individual choices, the practical means adopted to achieve them cannot vary with similar licence, for such means can be right or wrong. A practical reason has therefore to convey something that is true (at least ultimately true) for if false the reason given would suggest a means irrelevant to or incapable of producing the desired end. However, the truth in question need not be an 'absolute' truth but can be 'relative', that is, relative to what in a certain state of knowledge is believed or accepted as true. Where the participants in an argument believe in spirits, in a society (let us say) that generally shares 'ghostly' beliefs, they can still argue rationally, as they can argue according to what, for them, are 'objective' standards of what is true or false. The so-called 'primitive' trying to propitiate the gods is acting perfectly rationally, even intelligently, taking account of what he knows; what distinguishes him from modern man is his knowledge, not his head or rationality. Practical reasons thus possess a pronounced relativity depending entirely on the knowledge we have or deem sufficient to guide our actions towards our personal ends. And it is this very practicality of practical reasons, always concerned with what we need *to do*, that makes us speak of them as 'right' or 'wrong' rather than as 'true' or 'false', although truth and falsehood always remain in the background as the final arbiters of the success or failure of our means.

The practical reasons so far considered are perhaps best exemplified by those that appear in (what we may call) technical rules which tell us when or how to use certain objects or how to make certain things or how to bring about certain results. To ask when or why I should take an umbrella, or take this medicine, is asking what these things are for, whether they can serve my purposes in particular situations such as rain or sickness. To ask how I am to make certain things often calls for answers a little more complex because more manipulative: to make bread you have (roughly) to make and bake dough; to make an omelette you have to break, beat and cook eggs; the 'made' results now consist of natural facts not in their immediate but in mediated form, being 'made-up' or artificial results, artefacts 'constituted' by a combination of other things. Though nature provides chickens and eggs, it does not provide omelettes ready-made, nor for that matter the frying-pans in which they are cooked. Furthermore, technical rules, provided they are followed fairly correctly, offer a sort of truth-claim that a particular result can be said to exist. So we can say 'yes, this dish is an omelette', for we are stating certain propositions the truth or false-hood of which will depend on whether certain facts are the case, and in particular whether a specified set of acts has been performed. The proof of the omelette may not lie in the eating, for the alleged dish may taste quite un-omelette-like; yet provided the specified performances have been completed, it is, as we revealingly say, 'technically' an omelette, however untypical its appearance or taste.

Technical rules, to repeat, in no way order us to make bread or break eggs, they only convey that if bread or an omelette is what we want, then there are certain things it is necessary to do. Or they may still more simply convey an ordinary home-truth such as, 'these houses ought to be heated if it is desired to make them habitable'.[3] It is in this conditional sense, therefore, that we 'must' or 'have to' do certain things; also in this sense such rules are knowledgeable 'instructions' as well as (in Kant's phrase) 'hypothetical imperatives'. A particular feature of rules, then, is that they combine descriptive and prescriptive elements. A rule is obviously not solely descriptive as it would be were it confined merely to stating certain necessary conditions or causes and effects irrespective of the attainment of personal ends. Still the descriptive element here looms very large, not alone because we cannot disregard the factual component without which we would not know what the rule is about, but also because the instruction must connect with a true or verifiable proposition, for unless the descriptive part is correct, the rule would turn out to be inoperative or self-destructive: one would be telling somebody to do something that in fact cannot be done. Technical rules, in other words, translate theoretical into practical knowledge so as to adapt, as it were, the former for immediate personal use.

However not all our technical or practical knowledge can be stated confidently in certain reasons or rules. For there often are extraneous or supervenient factors which may falsify a result stated or predicted by a rule. Hence, being less certain or more fallible, we will surround the rule with cautious or cautionary reservations, that is we will add to it a *ceteris paribus* clause expressing a sort of hope of 'other things being equal' without really specifying what these other things could be; or we add a circumspect generalisation that it is only 'usually' or 'generally' that the specified result will obtain. Sometimes we translate these cautions by the word 'ought', as when we say that 'the water ought to boil in ten minutes' since this is the time it takes 'as a rule', or when we use 'ought' counterfactually as in 'the water ought to (would) have boiled but did not', the explanation being that other factors (a leaky kettle, a power-failure) intervened. These 'oughts' are purely descriptive, for they do not tell one what one has to do but merely what one can expect to be the case.[4] As such, again, they do not impugn the law of nature that water boils at a certain temperature but merely warn us about possibly adverse circumstances which that law may, for the sake of an overall generality or simplicity, conveniently leave out.

Somewhat similar considerations apply even where 'ought' resumes its characteristically prescriptive role, as where we seek practical answers to what are known as 'appetitive' questions, when we ask not just what we should do in relation to general or familiar results, but what we should do to satisfy our own very personal ends in the best possible way.[5] As the answer to this will depend on the circumstances of each questioner, including his special aptitudes or tastes, a useful answer cannot (normally) just consist of a general rule; we now have to offer some more particularised advice. Suppose A asks B about a particularly good restaurant to go to or about the most suitable profession to adopt; and suppose B's 'you ought to go to "The Gourmet"' expertly answers the first query, while 'you ought to become a lawyer' is good advice for the second; here the 'ought' in either answer, though again prescriptive, is however not just a polite imperative also designed to coincide with what B thinks A would like best. B may certainly hope that his answer will be well received by A, but his 'ought' implies distinctly more: it implies that B has a further reason for his prescription, namely that all people with A's tastes or capabilities would generally find The Gourmet or the Law eminently appropriate choices for their wants. B's 'ought', in other words, by no means avoids 'objective' scrutiny; it is as though B were telling A: 'you will find that my advice is right', just as right as where he said to A: 'you ought to bake the bread a little longer if you want it exactly the way you seem to like best'. Appetitive questions are then not unlike questions about acquiring skills; both respond to expert opinion, both invite specially adapted technical reasons which it would be somewhat awkward, and given their special nature even pointless, to translate into more general rules.

INSTITUTIONAL RULES AND INSTITUTIONAL FACTS

The rules obtaining in institutional situations, though very different from technical rules, are in some respects nevertheless very similar to them. Just as a person may ask how he can boil water or make bread, so he can ask what one has to do in certain social relationships, or ask about established social practices or requirements. A new employee may inquire when, or what time in the morning, he is to begin work; the newly elected chairman of an association may ask what his duties involve; a child may ask what one does to be courteous or polite; while a person may ask how he can make a contract or a will, or what he has to do to get married, and so on. In all these cases the questioner is seeking information or instruction as to how he can bring about a certain result: how he is to fulfil his role as an employee or chairman, or how he is to become polite or become a contractor or testator or a married spouse. The questioner knows that his new role or status consists of specified or specifiable acts or performances such as, in the case of marriage going through a particular ceremony; what he does not know is what precisely he must do to make this ceremony be the case.

It follows that what the questioner asks is: 'what have I technically to do?' He does not ask: 'what ought I to do?' or, 'what should I really do?' He does not ask the latter question because in the present context his concern is not *whether* he ought to perform his new role, but only *how* he is to perform it, since he accepts, or at the very least pretends to accept, the particular role such as it is. The position would be much the same if he were asking how he might play a particular piece by Bach and were then shown the relevant score. Obviously he will have to play that score as faithfully as possible if he is to play that piece at all; yet nobody, least of all Bach, has required him to play the piece however much our musician has to follow the score that Bach composed.

As in technical rules, again, institutional rules state or specify how we can bring about complex or 'artificial' results, except that institutional rules will specify not so much a combination or mixture of objects as rather a set of acts or performances. Thus to get married is to bring together a set of acts which, if fully completed, become an effective marriage ceremony. Seen in this way, marriage is as much an artefact as an omelette as it too is only brought about by observing the 'technical' constituents that make up this complex or constructive result; moreover it is a result to which a truth-value can be assigned, in that we can say 'yes, it is true that A and B were (or are) married' simply because the phrase 'to be married' implies that certain rules have been observed by making a set of events be the case. Not that the conclusive 'proof' of the marriage only lies in the specified ceremony; for the ceremony in question may, owing to other rules (some of which we refer to later) prove to be nugatory or without effect, being (for example) a bigamous association, although, as will quickly be obvious, we cannot even have a notion of bigamy unless A and B can 'create' a marriage in the first place, by going through certain performances. Institutional rules like technical rules, it is then clear, contain special bits of information offering practical answers to practical questions when we deliberate upon our choices or actions, namely, whether to do this or not to do it, or whether to do this or something else.

There nevertheless are very obvious differences between technical and institutional rules, differences closely corresponding to those between natural and social or (in current philosophical idiom) between 'brute' and 'institutional' facts. One crucial difference is that technical rules concerned with brute or natural facts have an 'objective' or invariable quality as they express a necessary connection between certain facts and other facts. Hence, for example, some such dish as an omelette must result if we observe the rules whether we call it an omelette or by some other name or even give it no name at all. On the other hand the rules applying to social or institutional facts do not possess the same sort of causal necessity since we can easily alter the rules concerning a marriage ceremony or making a will; institutional facts thus are peculiarly capable of being regulated as we may always introduce new rules specifying new acts or forbearances; indeed what gives certain facts their institutional character is just their social regulability. A law of nature, Aristotle said in a famous passage, admits of no variation and operates in exactly the same way everywhere—thus fire *burns* here and in Persia, while rules of justice (by which he meant not just legal but all kinds of social or conventional rules) keep changing before our eyes.[6]

Still, we must not drive the natural-conventional distinction too hard. Though true that conventional or institutional rules are, in principle, very alterable, utterly unlike technical rules, another explanation of this seems to have more to do with the fact that technical rules have to do with 'things' or 'products', whereas institutional rules are more concerned with 'activities', typically collaborative or cooperative activities involving two persons or more. Again, activities in their nature are regulable, unlike products which are not regulable but only makable. What is more, whereas products, once made, can be recognised by being seen or tested for what they are, activities cannot be similarly recognised for what they are or mean to achieve unless one knows the purpose or, if one prefers, the 'intention' of the observed activity. If we ask how certain brute or bare events (like exchanging words at a marriage ceremony or kicking or throwing balls in a game) can be recognised as institutions (as either a marriage ceremony or a game), or if we ask, to put this more generally, how brute facts can acquire institutional character, we would have no real answer unless we knew what the activity is about and, in particular, what sorts of wants or desires they pursue. For since an act (like exchanging words) does not declare itself as 'brute' or 'institutional', let alone declare its ultimate design, and since, furthermore, what we are watching is not a simple activity (like walking, eating, swimming etc.) but a complex one, being one of a set of different acts, we would still not know what a person is doing if we did not know, independently, what it means to wish to share a life with another person (as in marriage), or to wish to exercise competitive skills (as in games). We must, speaking a little more formally, know something about the antecedent X in the conditional statement 'If you want X then you must do Y'; and we must know this if from the as yet incomplete performance of Y, we are to be able to infer that someone is in the process of achieving X simply because we know that X-ing consists of doing Y_1, Y_2 and all the other Ys that complete the X-set. We shall illustrate this further when we return shortly to the rules of games.

The natural-conventional distinction must not be driven too hard for another reason as well. This is that it is surely not always the case that conventions keep changing literally all the time, for, if so, conventions would become useless things as we would never be able to know or say what they are. Hence to concede that conventions are variable, even radically so, still does not mean that they cannot remain stable or unaltered for some, albeit a short or unpredictable, time, quite apart from the fact that (as we shall see more fully in Chapter 5) there are many conventions which because of their moral or normative anchorage are far less readily alterable than the word 'convention' would suggest. But, in any case, to the extent that social conventions do exist, whether in unaltered or in periodically altered form, they can and must, during their duration, yield the kind of practical information which we have seen technical rules convey; so to this extent, though only to this, social or conventional or institutional rules can and do operate rather like technical rules. Indeed the words 'institution' or 'institutional' do seem to refer to social practices which are significantly less changing than mere fashions are; they are practices with something of a historic life-span and durability. Without this stability, institutional rules could never be learned or considered *qua* rules, whether by lawyers or historians or anthropologists: we could never say, for example, that amongst ourselves the operative rules are such-and-such while in France or among the Samoans the corresponding rules are significantly otherwise.

THE RULES OF GAMES

There exists another account of institutional rules in general and of games in particular which we may pause briefly to discuss. This is the now well-known account of Searle's according to which the conversion from brute into institutional facts is mediated solely by what he calls 'constitutive rules', that is rules broadly to the effect that 'X counts as Y in context C'; so that while brute facts can be accommodated by institutional facts, the latter can only be explained in terms of constitutive rules; for if you take away the rules there is no institution, take away the institution and there is, for example, no marriage and no game.[7] According to this view, furthermore, constitutive rules create or define new forms of behaviour which are logically entirely dependent on rules: 'The rules of football or chess, for example, do not merely regulate playing football or chess, but as it were they create the very possibility of playing such games'.[8] Constitutive rules are thus not imperatives ('do X', 'ties will be worn') but are rather specifications or definitions which taking the form they do ('X counts as Y, or counts as Y in context C') become analytic, or 'almost tautological', in character.[9]

Now in some respects, it is quickly seen, such constitutive rules bear a close resemblance to the technical or rather institutional rules we have earlier been considering, particularly rules relating to positive and collaborative activities or practices. Yet in other respects the Searlian account seems apt to mislead, simply because constitutive rules being, as they admittedly are, only analytic specifications, cannot by themselves adequately explain the nature of games, let alone other institutional events or activities, this for the important reason we already hinted at, that it is the ends we want or seek that here matter, no less than the rules themselves. Even if we grant that games are 'created' by particular 'constitutive' rules, the basic question still is what it is — in games — that is so created by them. When we watch a game, we do not watch the rules, nor for that matter an institution, but rather a series of brute facts consisting of a competitive display of skills (kicking, hitting, throwing, catching balls), a competition designed to result in either side winning or losing, since winning, including the pleasure of winning, is the typical, if not always the only, desire of a game; it is what the players want, what their supporters come to cheer. The competition certainly needs rules that specify the sorts of skills to be engaged, together with the tests we need to separate the winners from the losers, which tests will be usually though by no means invariably quantitative ones, measurable or countable by (say) 'points' or 'hits' or 'runs'.

So far, then, the rules do not create *a* game, they merely tell us *how* to play or win one; for there can be as many different games as we can invent ways of both exercising and testing our competitive skills. The relevant rules, having to remain rules of games and not of some other activity, thus only determine the modalities but not the concept of a game: or, in other words, the rules only state the variable *kinds* of games, they do not identify what is constant or essential in them. What is constant are indeed certain brute elements such as the desire to pursue (or to watch) competitive skills coupled with a desire of achieving (or witnessing) a win. More importantly, unless we recognise these brute elements, we cannot understand what sort of activity a game is. For unless these brute elements (exercising skills, seeking a win) are present to some extent, it would be impossible to distinguish a competitive game from some other pastime such as a game of pure luck (roulette or dice) where instead of exercising one's skills one gambles on a (usually) small chance of winning against heavy odds, or from an activity such as an acrobatic or artistic performance we can enjoy for the skills they display without entertaining anything remotely resembling a desire for a win. Nor need these brute elements have the same force for all concerned. One player may say 'we won, but it was a boring game'; another that the game was 'uninteresting perhaps, still we won'. To one what matters is the skill shown or engaged; to the other the main thing is to be on the winning side.

The upshot is that the nature of a game lies at least as much in certain human desires as it lies in rules. The boy who says to another 'let me race you to the corner' is not so much concerned with creating a new form of activity as he is concerned to come first, to be faster than the other boy. It is true that to enable one of them to be judgeable as the faster boy they will have to agree on the distance or stretch of their contest, for without such an agreement theirs would be just like the hare-and-tortoise race which, being (as it was perhaps supposed to be) unlimited and infinite, neither could win as neither could be said to come first. To this extent, the boys must agree to certain rules of their game, rules specifying the collaborative nature of their competition and the criteria for coming first; but this apart, the *aim* of the exercise is winning or losing: so much at least they must know *before* they make rules, as they must know what it means to seek or to compete for an advantage, what it feels to gain a victory or to suffer defeat. And this knowlege is not created by rules, but is a psychological or cognitive datum on which the rules build. This too may explain how we can play games even without rules, the sort of games children play when they improvise criteria according to which one loses, the other wins. Only organised or publicised games require rules, though even these remain changeable: there are several variations of football or draughts.

We begin to see more clearly what rules of games do and do not do. Classifiable as institutional or social rules, they represent of course collaborative practices that people pursue, as they represent a shared willingness between two players or two teams to engage in competitive skills. On the other hand, rules of games share some features of technical rules in that they provide not only specifications of the skills to be exercised but also tests or criteria to grade these skills, since without such grading criteria the skills applied would not be measurable and unless measurable could never issue in a win or loss. Games are also unlike institutional rules in another respect: unlike the latter they do not ultimately depend on social or heteronomous regulation, but depend at all times on the willingness of the participants. Indeed this applies to all sorts of other institutional activities, however many participants are involved, provided all of them willingly participate in a common programme of (broadly) collaborative tasks, whether they play games or run a voluntary society or play in an orchestra or whatever other multilateral activity they devise. The wish to collaborate must come from the participants themselves if, though only if, they at least broadly agree on the common result or end to pursue. The rules merely tell them how these common or collaborative results are to be pursued or achieved. Of course there remain a very large number of social activities which are not simply left to the autonomous decisions of the agents themselves. This however raises quite different questions as we shall shortly see.

AUTONOMOUS AND HETERONOMOUS RULES

It will have been noticed that practical reasons or rules can guide or influence actions in two crucially different ways, thus inviting a distinction between two sorts of rules we shall now describe (admittedly not altogether happily) as 'autonomous' and 'heteronomous', using these words not in a Kantian but a more traditional sense according to which autonomous rules are observed voluntarily or 'at will' while heteronomous rules are followed on order or command.[10] The former tell us how to achieve our ends or results, that is, our technical or institutional results, yet leave the decision whether or not to pursue them to our own ('autonomous') control; autonomous rules thus are self-guiding, or action-guiding in the way a blind man is guided by his dog, the blind man being willingly guided, the dog serving his purposes. By contrast, heteronomous rules guide action by directly regulating or prescribing acts or activities, thus overriding our freedom or autonomy. Heteronomy, as we are now using the word, does not mean that the rule has to be compulsory or coercive (though it can be that too), only that it is not indifferent as to its compliance and that it implies at least some social blame with or without a demand for an excuse for its breach. It is one thing to follow a 'Do not smoke'-rule autonomously for reasons of one's health; it is another thing to comply with a heteronomous 'No Smoking' sign. Unlike autonomous rules where non-compliance merely means that a desired result will not be achieved, heteronomous rules rather operate like imperatives as they serve directive or regulative purposes. Unlike autonomous rules, in other words, which you have to catch up with if you wish to attain your ends, heteronomous rules have a way of catching up with you, they will not leave you alone.

Unless we make some such distinction as between autonomous and heteronomous rules, and concomitantly between two kinds of prescriptivity, our common deontic expressions as 'must', 'ought', 'have to' remain confusingly ambiguous. In the case of autonomous rules such as those of games these expressions tell us what we 'must', 'have' or 'are' to do. Yet we do not say, in playing chess, that we are under an 'obligation' or 'duty' to move our pieces in certain ways, the rules only tell us how we are to play the game, assuming we wish to play it, so that the only question is whether our move is a valid one given the existence of certain rules.[11] Occasionally we may be told what we 'ought' to do, as when we inquire whether our move, though valid, is also a good one; we may be informed that we could or ought to have played it better by playing it differently, assuming the aim is to win. But this latter 'should' or 'ought' again does not express an obligation, it is rather like a technical suggestion or technically expert advice as to the skill we either have shown ourselves to lack or might acquire by recognising our mistake. In either case, however, it is up to the player whether he plays or how well he plays; the expressions 'must', 'have to' or 'ought' clearly retain their autonomous quality.

In the case of heteronomous rules, on the other hand, the nature of 'must', 'have to' or 'ought' is more forcibly prescriptive, for as regulations their purpose is precisely to impose duties or obligations by limiting our freedom of action either *vis-à-vis* all persons or only persons of a certain status or class. The rules pertaining to marriage, to take but

one example, restrict our freedoms as regards our roles as
husband or wife. Though initially we are free to marry or not
to marry as we wish, once we are married there are a number
of things we 'must', 'have to' or 'ought' to do, various
'obligations' we come under, various 'rights' we bestow, for
the benefit mainly of other persons, here the members of our
family. 'You must not or ought not to commit adultery',
'you ought to support your children' are rules only applicable
to certain people, but they are applicable with the same force
to them as the rule 'you must not steal' is applicable to
anybody irrespective of status, marital or otherwise. It
follows that the deontic expressions 'must' or 'ought'
function in their action-guidance quite differently according
to whether the context is autonomous or heteronomous. In
the former they guide us towards a more informed or more
successful choice. In the latter they communicate a requirement of compliance; instead of offering a choice, they create
obligations or duties as well as rights. Indeed the point of
heteronomous rules is that they are meant to be kept,
precisely because they represent a social desire to make the
world, or rather a particular human group, something other
than it is, at least in respect of some of its activities.

The autonomous-heteronomous distinction we have
drawn may help with a particular difficulty of the word
'ought'. It has recently been maintained that just as the rules
of chess require us to move our pieces in certain ways, so the
institutional rules relating to (for example) promises require
us to adhere to certain obligations, in particular that of
keeping promises. What this overlooks is that the rules
concerning promises, though certainly institutional, are
nevertheless very different from the rules of games: different
because, as we have already seen, the latter rules depend on an
autonomous choice, whereas the rules relating to promises,
like virtually all other institutional rules with the one
exception of games, have also a heteronomous side. Hence it
seems a mistake to speak, as Searle has done, of the
'constitutive' rules of institutions as though this enabled us to

derive the same conclusions for both chess and promises (and so, incidentally, derive an 'ought' from an 'is'). It is a mistake because the characteristic use of 'ought' in promise-keeping is heteronomous, not autonomous as it is in certain other institutional rules, especially games. It is true that a person may sometimes wish to learn how the word 'promise' is or ought to be used, or what it normally implies; but this is a different matter which does not affect the present (heteronomous) uses of 'ought'.

In this light, again, it becomes misleading to regard institutional rules as 'constitutive' rather than 'regulative', it being concomitantly argued that these are the two major sorts of rules; misleading simply because this is only true of collaborative, and not of other, institutions which latter do maintain a difference between autonomous and heteronomous rules.[12] An Edwardian sign vividly illustrates this dual aspect of institutional rules: 'Ladies and Gentlemen will not, others must not, step on the grass'. Clearly if you (autonomously) behave like a lady or gentleman you 'will' not step on the grass; if you do not so behave you are in any case caught in the heteronomous net of all the 'others' who 'must' not step on the grass, whether they will or not.

As this example further shows, what is valuable in the constitutive-regulative distinction is anyhow absorbed by that between autonomous and heteronomous rules. In fact the constitutive-regulative distinction can be seen to be subsidiary or secondary to the autonomous-heteronomous one. The reason for this, as we shall now suggest, is that both autonomous and heteronomous rules can each be action-guiding in either a constitutive or regulative way. Thus an autonomous rule may be constitutive where it tells us how to play chess, yet seem regulative where we, self-guidingly, resolve to turn over a new leaf, to take cold showers, to go on a diet and so on. Of course heteronomous rules are, normally and typically, regulative as in 'do not kill', 'do not steal' etc., but they are occasionally also constitutive as in 'passports are invalid after a year'. In law there are indeed many rules which are constitutive rather than regulative in the sense that they are not directly or coercively sanctionable as are regulative legal rules but are 'sanctionable' rather by way of negating the validity of certain acts, as by invalidating a will or contract or by the cancellation or withdrawal of certain rights (e.g. a licence to trade), a consequence which may produce a disadvantage no less significant than a sanction consisting of a physical or financial penalty. Two people playing chess according to the 'wrong' constitutive rules may not be playing 'chess' but nevertheless another sort of game (say, 'chesso' or 'mini-chess') which as a game will be effective between the two players, since one of them will win, the other lose according to their modified or improvised rules of the game. However, two parties making a legally 'wrong' contract may be wholly disappointed in their attempt to change their respective positions; they will find that nothing has changed.

Yet there remains a special logical relationship between autonomous and heteronomous rules. So it is important to realise that if institutional rules can be looked at purely autonomously, the very possibility of this (excepting games and other such cooperative activities) depends directly on the prior existence of heteronomous rules. Consider again the statement 'Smith married Jones'. If we ask how exactly marriage becomes an institution or why the rules make it so, an initial answer would be that Smith and Jones went through a certain ceremony whereupon they acquired a new status, and so on. However if next we ask why it is that we need a special ceremony or why a special status comes about, we have to say considerably more. Obviously Smith and Jones cannot simply say or assert that they are married; getting or being married are not acts or activities that people simply living together engage in (like sharing a house, making love, having children), but are acts that are subject to special regulations of a positive and negative kind: negative in that people cannot marry everybody (brother or sister, parent or child) just as, once married, they cannot acquire an additional spouse; and positive in the sense that there are a number of specific obligations and claims between husband and wife, broadly those of cohabitation and mutual support. Unless, in other words, various heteronomous regulations are fulfilled, an institution like marriage cannot even get off the ground; it is they which establish the framework of the institution, including the particular acts or abstentions by virtue of which this institution becomes what it is. Indeed unless heteronomous rules first set up a pattern of obligations and rights, our marriage ceremony would have little or nothing to be a ceremony of.

Thus it is only because heteronomous rules can so regulate social conduct as to establish (in ways we shall have later to explain) fairly firm patterns of behaviour that these lend themselves to technical descriptions which we can know and learn as we can know and learn any other technical rules. To see this is particularly important for an understanding of legal rules which can assume an eminently technical and in a way even a 'scientific' character in a way that moral rules do not. We can say, for example, that we spent the last year learning, studying, working on legal rules, like learning or studying mathematics or chemistry. We cannot, at least we do not normally, say that we spent the last year learning moral rules, unless these moral rules have turned into settled practices or moral codes; but then we would refer to something very different; we would then speak of moral rules which are as detailed and established as legal rules typically are.

HETERONOMY AND RATIONALITY

We still have to consider in what sense heteronomous rules can be said to be rational. In autonomous situations a rational element is not hard to find. For here an agent's rationality is determined by whether he is guided by any reasons, and if so what reasons, in achieving or trying to achieve his ends, be they his own ends or the ends also of those with whom he acts. Here the rational question is always how effectively or correctly he acts to achieve his several or joint result; the success of an action is its best rational, just as it is its best empirical proof. In heternomous situations, however, a rational element is more difficult to identify; there are two quite separate aspects to be discussed. The first has to do with the rationality of having heteronomous rules at all: what is the use of saying that something 'has' or 'must' or 'ought' to be done? Obviously there would be little point in using or even having prescriptive or heteronomous language, or speech-acts with broadly imperatival effect, if the social pressure behind it were consistently negligible, or never likely to be complied with by the person or persons to whom the rules are addressed. To have rules then means that it makes sense to have them, that they are generally or frequently obeyed, that the social pressure is effective, at any rate within a given group.[13] Certainly the compliant effects of rules are not unlimited, though what these limits are is largely an empirical question which does not concern us now.

The second aspect, by far the more important for our purposes, raises a much wider problem perhaps best introduced by way of another question: how can we tell a 'perfect' criminal that he behaved 'rationally' because he was not caught but that he did not behave 'rationally' merely by dint of committing a crime: what, more particularly, is the meaning of 'rational' in the second sense? The full answer to this will only emerge gradually in the course of this book. At present we are still dealing with some preliminary yet quite fundamental points. First it is necessary to emphasise that our present rules, heteronomous though they are, yet remain *rules*, that is, they are imperative statements accompanied or justified by reasons. An absolutely heteronomous rule, one refusing to give any reason for itself, would hardly be classifiable as a rule, rather as an arbitrary command or imperative. Certainly all imperatives are action-guiding: 'stand up', 'shut up', or a robber's 'your money or your life' convey clear prescriptions which we are guided by and comply with if only because of the possible consequences if we do not; such imperatives are not simply noises designed to frighten us, they mean to order us; also, they are quite unlike phrases like 'damn' or 'hooray' which are not prescriptive but merely expressive of the speaker's particular feelings; instead of issuing such expletives he could just as well jump or scream or break into tears. Other commands, again, are somewhat less arbitrary in the sense that they introduce some, albeit a weak, rational element. A command may not be valid unless it comes down from some authority, as where the commander occupies an acceptedly superior position *vis-à-vis* the commanded. 'An order is an order' is not, in such a case, a totally arbitrary or irrational thing to say since the commander's superior position may itself have good reasons for it, except that in such an authoritarian relationship 'an order is an order' is the end of further discussion; the order, including any possible reasons for it, has now to be taken as read.

As we turn to moral or legal rules, however, the imperatival function can be further weakened, not to say submerged, leaving behind it little more than an action-guiding prescriptivity. In this way the imperative turns into a full-fledged rule; moreover it is a rule which, like the other rules we have been considering, invites consideration of its substantive content in that it does invite (implicitly if not explicitly) the rule-subject to ask for or question the reasons for it, or to offer his own reason or justification or excuse for the breach of a rule. Indeed the reasons accompanying a rule are reasons which a rule-subject is, so to speak, invited to share. The genuine law-abiding citizen, for example, abides by a social or moral rule because he understandingly accepts that he 'ought' to comply, not because he obediently submits to certain 'don'ts' or 'musts'; at the very least he can understand the purpose or content of the rule which is precisely why we cannot have rule-discourse with uncomprehending individuals such as small infants or lunatics. All this of course closely connects with another logical point, namely, that ought-statements can, while straightforward imperatives cannot, be used unassertively as where we say, in *oratio obliqua*, 'I suppose he ought to do this' or 'I don't hold that he ought to do that'; full imperatives are always assertive as they cannot be supposed or believed.[14]

Of course the rule, for all its rationality, yet remains heteronomous because, for one thing, it is still practical or action-guiding, the guidance operating in a social context of pressure that comes from and serves the group as a whole; and because, for another thing, such a rule differs from a piece of advice or from a mere opinion or prayer that something is or be the case. Advice and opinions, too, require the giving of reasons why the advice or opinion tendered is good or sound, otherwise we could never distinguish between good and bad, sound and unsound advice etc.; but the point is that it is for the person to accept or reject advice as he pleases, whereas the reasons advanced as part of heteronomous rules cannot be simply rejected precisely because they are heteronomous, not autonomous. Indeed, as we shall later see in greater detail, the heteronomous rule can only be 'trumped', as it were, by counter-reasons amounting to a denial or qualification of the reasons given for the rule. So it becomes clear that the heteronomous rule stands somewhere midway between a command and advice; it is both distinctly less than a pure command and distinctly more than just an opinion: we may perhaps call it a 'reasonable' imperative because it invites discussion, dialogue, argument or (in short) reasoning between the two sides.

However to say all this is still not quite enough. In particular, it is not enough to say that rules give or invite reasons, for we still have to say what these reasons are and, more especially, how these reasons work out in an argument. We are not now giving reasons or counter-reasons about facts (which, for example, we would be if we were discussing the soundness or otherwise of a particular technical rule), but are rather giving reasons and counter-reasons in terms of obligations and excuses, that is, arguing about the moral 'value' of an action in terms of the grievances or excuses to which an action may give rise. Hence the reasons we give for our actions cannot simply take the form of an exchange of charge and counter-charge; rather they need to become like stepping-stones in an argument which convinces not just because it persuades sentimentally (persuades the passions, as Hume might say), but convinces because the argument has or can be shown to have some degree of finality or concludability. In other words, just as a technical argument has rational strength because it is concludable according to empirical criteria, including the truth-value of the propositions on which it is based, so an argument about the moral 'value' of an action needs to be underpinned by some standard or standards in terms of which such an argument can be carried on and possibly finalised. For the only logical justification of bringing technical and moral or legal rules within a category of 'rules' is that they all share at least this one feature, that they all lend themselves to argument which can be either right or wrong. We shall later suggest that to show how people can argue intelligibly with each other about their obligations or claims, we must first understand how certain reasons become moral reasons, or certain rules moral rules, as well as how moral rules can settle into moral practices; all of which, indeed, will give us a better understanding also of the ultimate foundations of legal reasoning. But for the present we still have to deal with various other problems to prepare the ground for things to come.

2 Moral and Prudential Considerations

PRUDENTIAL REASONING: MEANS AND ENDS

We will have seen that rules are action-guiding in a distinctly rational way since they offer, or at least imply, the existence of reasons or criteria in the light of which we can argue as well as judge whether our actions are right or wrong, or correct or incorrect. We now have to see that these reasons differ greatly according to whether they support actions on prudential or on moral grounds, the first type of reasons serving our self-chosen or self-regarding aims, the second more essentially other-regarding, being reasons why we must or must not do certain things regardless of whether or not they coincide with our own wants or interests.[1] This prudential-moral distinction extends and complements, but in some ways also cuts across, that between autonomous and heteronomous rules. One may comply with a 'no smoking' sign because one is (autonomously) impressed by the medical fact that smoking is a health hazard; or alternatively because one is (heteronomously) impressed either by the threat of a penalty in which case one acts prudentially, in one's own interest, or because of purely moral considerations for other people's health. Legal rules, in particular, comprise both such moral and prudential elements. Without a prudential element we could not explain how legal rules can persuade or 'coerce' us to do what they tell us to do, while without a moral component legal rules would have no sense of direction and be just an aggregate of penalty-threatening

24

imperatives. To this matter we return in Chapter 6; our more immediate task is to examine some basic aspects of prudential reasoning, and especially how prudential reasons compare with moral ones.

Consider again the 'perfect' criminal adverted to earlier. The man who commits the 'perfect' crime behaves both rationally and prudently if he adopts appropriately effective means for accomplishing his purposes. He is rational not of course as regards the criminal end he sets himself, for we are assuming, as now we have to assume, that our human aims and ends being free, he need not give reasons for this: he is rational rather in that he deliberates about the available means to attain his end, weighing the risks of failure against the chances of success. The criminal would behave irrationally as well as imprudently were he to act without regard for the attainability of his end, either by disregarding the appropriate means to be adopted or, in a wider sense, by failing to adjust or even to limit or qualify his end, if necessary radically, if the available means reveal the end to be impossible or impracticable of attainment, or if the available or practicable means prove too unrealistic or too costly, having regard to the satisfaction he hopes to derive from the realisation of his enterprise. To act rationally or prudentially is then to act with due regard to available means as these relate to achievable ends, just as to act without such regard is to act irrationally or imprudently as well as imperfectly or unwisely or foolishly.

But the words 'prudential' and 'rational', though often used interchangeably, do not always mean quite the same. While every prudential action is also rational, not every rational action is prudent as well. If 'rational' thus is the wider notion, what does it denote more specifically? The broad answer is that rationality not only implies giving reasons but, more particularly, reasons that can be described as either right or wrong. For to argue rationally, we earlier pointed out, is to give reasons in order to clinch or conclude an argument, the conclusion lying precisely in a sort of acceptable verdict that the argument is right or wrong, the right-wrong dichotomy ensuring that the reasons given are 'objective' reasons, or reasons that are, so to speak, independent or external or superior to ourselves, as distinct from reasons which might be described as purely internal, based on our personal feelings or passions, reasons which do not lend themselves to argument, precisely because being entirely personal they withdraw from reasoning. The explanation why scientific criteria seem to us so preeminently rational, as almost the prototype of rationality, is then simply that scientific or technical criteria provide the most accessible or manageable forms of concludability as they are factually or observationally testable; empirical testability offers an independent or external method by which an argument can be finalised in a relatively definite way. 'Rational' is thus not merely another word for 'logical', 'plausible', 'commonsensical' and so on; rationality indicates a basic procedure for resolving arguments we take to be capable of being right or wrong; an irrational argument accordingly is not merely wrong, its real trouble is that it is not even wrong.

Prudent or prudential considerations, too, include the deliberation of means for ends, but they also include a consideration of how good or effective or successful these means are. To be regarded as prudent, our 'perfect' criminal has to employ what are, if not ideally at any rate optimally, the 'best' means for his objective, those means as to minimise the risks of failure and maximise the chances of success. 'Best' being a comparative word, it implies a possible choice from among various or alternative means, especially where there are, even in connection with one project or enterprise, quite a few different ways of achieving that end. None of this means however that we have to eschew all known or possible risks. If one objects that our so-called 'perfect' criminal is acting imprudently or unwisely as he is still running some risk of being found out, the answer is that provided this possibility is sufficiently remote, his crime, though perhaps in one sense no longer 'perfect', would not be any the less prudently rational.

Many, perhaps most, of our actions are never completely 'prudent' to the extent of being strictly fool-proof; if things had to be done with complete security, we could never prudently travel by car, or plane, taking into account the (statistically) by no means negligible possibility of death or injury such means of transport entail. Similarly to invest money, though sometimes a hazardous enterprise, becomes an acceptable risk if undertaken with care. Not that even a prudent investment will always succeed; it may turn out badly because of bad luck or because of unforeseeable circumstances which intervene, yet we would still describe it as a 'reasonable' or prudent action, if the risk taken is acceptable according to the conventional wisdom by which these things are judged.

It may not be generally realised that prudent or prudential actions are not necessarily selfish ones. Where a gunman says 'your money or your life', you may think it advisable to submit, yet the victim is still not acting strictly selfishly in surrendering the money, just as a person is not acting selfishly even as he acts prudently where he decides to give up smoking in the light of all the medical evidence. To act prudently is primarily to act wisely, or intelligently, not foolishly, in the furtherance of one's own aims or interests, always assuming that this aim is to stay alive (as the gunman's victim) or to remain healthy (as in the smoker's example). In the gunman's case, even if the victim refused to do as ordered, apparently nothing would be gained since the gunman, if true to his threat, would still rob and kill. Yet to the extent that the victim does have a choice between living and dying, he can still be said to act self-regardingly but not, strictly, selfishly. In this sense it seems true, as Singer says, that prudence is neither moral nor immoral; though it seems less true that prudence must be distinguished, as he also claims, from egoism since prudence 'is more like rational or enlightened self-interest than it is like mere self-interest which may be shortsighted and unenlightened'.[2] In the first place, even the most selfish and perhaps 'unenlightened' action, like that of the 'perfect' criminal, may be done completely prudently in achieving the given aim; egoism is thus not imprudent or irrational *per se*. A truer difference between an enlightened and an unenlightened action is not that one is rational or prudent, the other irrational or imprudent, but rather that an enlightened action (as we shall shortly further see) envisages the interests of citizens in general. In the second place, what does distinguish prudence from egoism is that the latter seeks the realisation of one's own ends however much these may compete or conflict with other people's interests; prudence has more to do with the deliberative care or caution with which an action is or should be performed, it being often but not always the case that the action is entirely for one's own purposes.

This self-regarding feature brings to light another subtle difference between prudence and rationality. Since as free men it is not irrational for us to adopt such ends as we wish, we may adopt even ends which, instead of beneficial or advantageous, may be ruinous or destructive of ourselves. For, as Hume said, 'it is not contrary to reason for me to choose my total ruin', nor 'contrary to reason to prefer the destruction of the whole world to the scratching of my finger'.[3] Certainly I would be acting irrationally were the world's destruction to bring worse consequences to me than would the scratch; but if I were clear in my own mind what the destruction entails, yet still preferred it, I would be acting rationally in adopting the right means to bring it about. Even so it is distinctly odd to say that performing one's self-destruction constitutes a prudent or prudential act, precisely because the word 'prudence' normally refers to the re-alisation of self-serving or life-enhancing interests, not to destructive steps which would bring all self-regarding interests to an irrevocable end. Be this as it may, the termination of a life need not be regarded as an irrational or imprudent thing to do. The wise man, in the Stoic view, would opt for suicide if there was sufficient reason such as great suffering or great pain. This, we may add, was not

Kant's view; for him, some personal ends do derive from reason, there being certain ends that every rational person, by virtue merely of his rationality, must necessarily will; thus he cannot rationally will to commit suicide or let his talents remain idle or unrealised.[4] Not only is this the weakest part of Kant's doctrine (why, for example, should a man of leisure not feel self-realised?), it does not, as we shall later see, even follow from Kant's own canon of moral judgement, the categorical imperative.

PRUDENCE, BENEVOLENCE AND MORALITY

We have been considering prudential actions as the 'best' means of achieving our strictly self-regarding ends, those dominated by our own particular interests. However, prudential actions can also be other-regarding, intended to benefit other persons rather than oneself. Such prudent actions are sometimes imposed by law as where a trustee is required to manage another's affairs with particular care. For present purposes, however, the more significant cases are those where one person wishes to benefit another in a kindly or benevolent way because he is generous by nature or because he feels identified with the desires or interests of the person he wishes to benefit. In the latter case a benefactor may even feel quite unhappy if his desire to be kindly remained unfulfilled. Again, suppose you know that doing X will make another person (A) miserable; here you may refrain from X-ing for both a prudent and a moral reason: a prudent one in that you wish A to be happy as this gratifies your own desires, and a moral reason in that A's welfare happens to be important to you. There are, fortunately for society, many situations in which prudential considerations coincide or conjoin with moral concerns; unless this were so co-operative or collaborative activities would scarcely occur.[5]

This must however not create the impression that prudential and moral considerations are apt to collapse into each other, or that because of this special connection morality even 'works' or 'pays' in a distinctly prudential way. Consider the example of the Prisoners' Dilemma where just this is supposed to be the case. Two prisoners, having jointly committed a crime, are to be tried if the prosecution can assemble enough evidence against them, including a confession from one or both. Now if (1) both confess they will each get ten years (a reduced punishment); if (2) neither confesses, they only get two years for another crime for which there is sufficient evidence; if (3) only one confesses, the confessor goes free, but the other gets twenty years (the full penalty).[6] Confronted by this choice, each prisoner, acting just for himself, decides to confess; each gets therefore ten years instead of two years had he said nothing; they are thus both worse off despite their individually rational and prudential behaviour. Had they behaved morally, the argument goes, had they mutually kept faith about not confessing, they would each have been better off, getting only two years instead of ten. Still, this example does not go very far: it only shows that the respective chances or utilities may sometimes be so distributed that moral and prudential considerations completely coincide; the example certainly does not prove that while self-interested conduct typically leads to disutility, morality always or even normally 'pays'; there are life-situations enough where one's self-interest only too clearly conflicts with the dictates of morality. And, in any case, since as in this example morality only 'pays' if the prudential odds are in its favour, morality becomes quite indistinguishable from prudential interests. However a prudential morality of this kind amounts to no more than an expedient morality, a morality perhaps only worthy of the hypocrite who, honouring the price that vice pays to virtue, only chooses to be moral as it pays to be so.

As we have benevolent feelings for another person so we may have such attitudes for a group or community as a whole; we may wish to benefit not just specific persons like relatives or friends, or a small group like a team, but a large class of persons, including strangers, a class possibly embracing a whole society. Our benevolent ideal may here seek to do what is 'best' or 'good' for all, or for most or many of the community, to do things like controlling pollution, or improving public health, or enhancing the quality of life. Such enlightened ideals may flow from basic moral attitudes, including a deep respect for humanity; alternatively, they may be purely prudential, inspired mainly by an acute sense of social expediency. Many of our political measures strive for just such expedient reforms; political argument, too, often turns out to be prudential just in this expedient sense, the argument characteristically being about the 'best' means available to achieve the socio-economic improvements for which people might vote. In other words just as I can, prudentially or expediently, deliberate about the best means to promote *my* welfare, so we can think of *our* welfare, our group's or society's. Indeed all this brings us very near to utilitarianism, at any rate in the version propounded by Professor Smart.[7] Assuming we are all benevolent men, we know soon enough why we take action A rather than action B, the 'simple and natural' reason being that doing A will make mankind happier than B, so that given this benevolent aim, all we have to consider is whether, or how, our actions will contribute to general human happiness. Smart admits that we cannot calculate exactly all the consequential advantages of our actions, that we do not possess 'precise methods for deciding what to do'; hence even 'imprecise methods must just serve their turn'. In other words, a utilitarian approach does no more than provide 'a criterion for rational choice'; and we are asked to make the same rational choice 'in the field of ethics' as we make in respect of our private concerns.[8]

Yet, again, it will be clear that being thus benevolent or kindly does not exhaust the meaning of morality. Not because benevolence is a non-moral or amoral attitude; nor because one would deny that such benevolence, where it exists, will tend to give us the effects of morality as it may well contribute to greatly improved human relationships. The point rather is that being benevolent or altruistic are mainly contingent dispositions. Only angels with their 'holy wills' are necessarily benevolent, only they can be un-exceptionally relied upon never to act unkindly. The rest of us can and do act more selfishly, often enough without the least benevolent disposition, if only because men can be the moral victims of their own rationality: they may think or even show it to be far more advantageous for themselves to act unjustly or immorally: an act that harms others is not *eo ipso* against reason. Conversely, we can be moral, or at least say that we ought to be moral, without feeling in the least kindly or benevolent. Indeed even assuming we all were benevolent, this would not make it even approximately clear what, concretely, this benevolence commits us to. Grievances or disputes continue to be possible; consequently we shall still need some sort of theory as to how various moral claims or grievances could be met or in any case argued or reasoned about. Purely empirical or prudential con-siderations cannot fully meet this need.

MORAL ENDS AND RATIONALITY

It follows that in the end we are again caught in the Humean dilemma that to be moral is to be something other than just being rational in the sense of being prudent and intelligent.[9] For just as reason may help us to realise our benevolent or kindly intentions, it may also serve our selfish or immoral desires. Again, as reason does not dictate our personal or prudential objectives, so it does not prescribe our moral ends. Such familiar moral teachings as 'love thy neighbour' or 'the greatest virtue is charity' or 'a decency is required' (in Browning's poetic phrase), though admittedly far from inappropriate prescriptions for moral behaviour, are by no means rationally self-evident, being rather what moral emotivists would call 'persuasive' appeals or entreaties. In fact the important contribution of emotivism here has been to remind us to take Hume seriously, though to take him seriously makes the task of showing a logical connection between reason and morality even more difficult; still unless one does proceed from a Humean position one simply fails to take account of an absolutely central difficulty in morals. Even so, to come to terms with Hume need not be the end but can be the beginning of a workable view of moral rationality.

To adumbrate such a view let us begin with the point made earlier that while reason guides or instructs us as to the means we have to adopt to achieve our ends, in doing this it sometimes throws not inconsiderable light on these ends themselves. It does so in two ways: it throws light on the attainability or practicability of a given end, including the qualifications this end must undergo if it is to be achievable by practically available means. Secondly, and more broadly, reason throws light on ends inasmuch as the practical reasons we give for our actions, though they primarily concern means, are yet about means which are judgeable according to their end-effectiveness since they are judgeable as right or wrong means in relation to particular ends. Thus even though our ends are indeed free, and not directly dictated by reason, they are nonetheless not immune from rational deliberation; for the reasons we give, though means-oriented, must be the end-effective as well, however much the rationality of prudential reasons lies predominantly in the 'best' means of achieving ends. As we turn to moral reasons, however, our business is not so much with 'factual' means, not because moral rules exclude facts (moral rules are not less fact-saturated than other rules), as rather because moral reasons switch from means to ends, being more directly concerned with ends than with means. A moral statement like 'you did wrong to do hurt' or 'you did right to help' is a statement about *what* you ought to do, not about *how* to act for the purpose of hurting or helping. Similarly the 'perfect' criminal we encountered earlier is judged or condemned not for the 'perfection' of his crime, for we may indeed admire his successful means; he is morally or legally condemned for the 'criminality' of his end. Prudential and moral reasons thus follow quite different, if sometimes parallel, paths; nor is there a giant step we can take to bridge the gulf between them. Prudential reasons, with their emphasis on means, seek to *explain* our actions *qua* means to ends; moral reasons, with their emphasis on ends, have to *justify* our actions precisely in terms of their ends.

The great question therefore is how, or from what point of view, moral ends can be considered to be rational ends. One or two things should now be a little clearer than before. The first is that our moral ends will have to be, or be shown to be, socially shared or sharable ends, that is, ends which are not just our own ends but ends that relate also to the ends of others, so as to make them mutually compatible or trans-personal ends. In the moral field rational analysis is therefore primarily about how one's own ends can relate to as well as integrate with another person's ends. Another thing now may also be a little clearer: that these sharable ends must be shown as not simply happening to be shared, as not merely contingently or autonomously shared ends, but shown as ends which, so to speak, *must* be shared if we are to be able to argue, especially concludably argue, about our inter-personal grievances. As our business now is with grievances that arise because our mutual ends are in collision or conflict (as where, to take a typical case, my end to remain unharmed has been disturbed by your action taken in pursuit of your own end or interests), it follows that moral rationality becomes a logical quest for the conditions that here determine a moral argument, including the conditions or presuppositions on the basis of which it becomes possible to debate and judge our grievances both morally and systematically; and in particular the two sorts of grievances that in human affairs can and so frequently do arise, namely grievances about the harm we do to each other or grievances about some mal-distribution of the goods of life. Thus, though we started with a strongly

Humean thrust, to the effect that both prudential and moral ends or aims in life do not derive from reason but derive instead from personal desires, we now arrive at a position that does suggest a closer connection between reason and morality; except that this is a connection in which reason is no longer taken in a cognitive sense, as a self-sufficient source of morality, but is given an analytical or self-reflective rôle: reason simply becomes our logical way of finding, or of constructing, a framework within which an orderly and concludable moral argument can be carried on. In this way, just as prudential rationality offers external or supra-personal criteria in terms of which the practical reasons we give for an action can be adjudged as being right or wrong, so in the moral field rationality now provides, in a comparable procedure, those external or independent standards without which we cannot reason about, let alone settle, our inter-personal grievances or complaints.

Yet it remains also true that these two procedures comparable in one respect are still very different in another. Where prudential rationality with its focus on the relation of means to ends ultimately relies on empirical experience, moral rationality with its emphasis on ends remains caught by the same difficulty with which the whole problem began, namely, that our human ends instead of being shared may actually diverge or collide, precisely because they are or have to be presumed to be free, for if unfree no problem could in fact arise. It is indeed just because of this central difficulty that reason now plays a non-cognitive even though a still vital logical part, its specific task now being (as already indicated) to examine the arguments we commonly advance to justify either our grievances or our actions, and to examine these arguments, above all, in the light of their particular social contexts and assumptions as well as of their systematic or concludable possibilities.

All this will occupy us at length in later chapters. For the present we are still concerned with the prudential-moral distinction, particularly as this distinction appears to have become somewhat blurred in a good deal of moral theory, not so much because the distinction is not recognised as, rather, because it is not always observed sufficiently sharply. It is even quite frequently assumed that moral judgments are, in the main, very much like prudential decisions in the sense that even moral decisions can be seen as personally autonomous. This immediately brings us to two famous arguments which have long claimed to provide an adequate 'personal' basis of morality. One is the Golden Rule Argument, the other Kant's Categorical Imperative.

THE GOLDEN RULE ARGUMENT

What is known as the Golden Rule Argument broadly asserts (to give it its negative which is also its more characteristic version) that you must not do to others what you would not have them do to you. Not only is this ancient wisdom (the pre-Socratics already had an argument of this kind), it is still today a useful educational device, there being perhaps no quicker way of making us realise, children especially, that one blow easily leads to another so that in the end nothing is gained. As a moral argument, however, there is a great deal wrong with it; it ends up as a prudential and *ad hominem* argument, as though the whole secret of morality lay in convincing a particular person to act in his own best interests.

How essentially prudential the golden rule argument in fact is can be seen in an example greatly relied on by Hare.[10] It will therefore be instructive to spend a little time on it. Suppose that A owes money to B, that B owes money to C, and that it is the law that creditors may exact their debts by putting their debtors into prison. Although B clearly wants his money back, he may yet ask himself whether he can morally send A to prison. B may remember that if he does, C may do the same to him, a consequence B may be most unhappy about. So what makes A's going to prison unattractive to B is the likelihood that he (B) will go also; the whole argument therefore rests on B's having no desire to go to prison for his own default. An indifferent or apathetic person, Hare adds, one not caring at all what happened to himself or others would not be touched by this argument, for this cannot work unless B does care, or is prepared to use his imagination to appreciate not just how he (B) would react to C's action but also how A would react to what he (B) does to A; for this purpose B would have to treat A's possible inclinations and reactions as if they were his own. Hare indeed regards this inclination and imagination essential 'ingredients' without which the whole argument would not work, although there are also two other ingredients, the requisite facts of the case, and the framework provided by the logical (universalisable) meaning of the word 'ought'; but it is clear that the former ingredients are now more essential than the latter two; it is they which, Hare maintains, 'turns selfish prudential reasoning into moral reasoning'.

Yet how good an instance is this of moral reasoning? Once we start with a person who refrains from hurting another because he knows what it is, or might be, to inflict suffering, we are no longer dealing with a 'selfish prudential' man but with one of kindly disposition, a person already morally inclined or morally committed; moreover, if B is not moved by his own imagination there is, on Hare's account, nothing else we can do: we cannot even tell him that he morally ought to refrain from inflicting suffering since the 'ought' is morally neutral as, on his account, the ought does not form part of any particular moral rule. Again, since B's imagination depends on his personal inclination not to suffer himself, Hare's golden rule argument, far from truly moral, reveals itself as more prudential in kind, since its 'foundation', as Hare revealingly says, is 'universalised self-interest'.[11] He insists, it is true, that this self-interest has to be universalised and thus consistently applied: accordingly B ought not to do to A what he wishes C ought not to do to him. But it is difficult to see how consistency here alters the case, for the consistency now in question is at most B's being consistent with himself. Nor is it at all clear why B needs to be regarded as inconsistent if he wants his money from A but still does not want to pay C. The case would be different if B pretended to act on or under a wider moral principle such that 'no one should suffer by going to prison merely because unable to pay his debt'. But this is not the tenor of the present argument. According to this if B can be said to be acting on a 'principle' at all, this would be one of his own making, inspired by his own self-interest or inclinations, a principle which therefore again seems more prudential than moral.[12]

This analysis is further strengthened by what Hare says next, namely by the escape-routes he allows to the morally indifferent and the fanatic. If a person says 'you have no right to judge me morally since nothing morally matters', this is the end of the moral dialogue; though, as Hare hastens to add, this need not disturb us, for just as one cannot play chess with an unwilling partner, so moral argument is impossible with someone refusing to enter into a moral dispute. Similarly, if a person happens to be a moral eccentric or fanatic he may even entertain views or ideals that may defy even his own self-interest. Suppose, to take Hare's example, B says that A ought to go to prison only because his skin is black or has a hooked nose, for 'it is always possible for a man to come to hold an ideal which requires that he himself be sent to a gas-chamber if a Jew. That is the price we have to pay for our freedom'.[13] A little reflection shows that this cannot do. As we have hinted before and shall argue again, it is the very function of moral rules to regulate our behaviour by restricting our freedom wherever necessary; their function is to provide reasons for saying that a free agent acts immorally if he inflicts unnecessary or avoidable suffering. For though we are free to act the way we want, we are not thereby freed from being morally judged or criticised. Thus the price we pay for our freedom is not the right to be morally indifferent or fanatic, the price we pay is our exposure to judgement according to rules, moral rules that distinguish 'right' from 'wrong' actions.

Indeed, even disregarding such monsters as the racial (or gas-chamber) fanatic, the fact is that in one way or another we may all be fanatics in the defence of our personal inclinations or interests: as sado-masochists, greedy employers, harsh landlords, extortionate money-lenders, cruel disciplinarians and so on, inflicting harm on other persons, but still (even sincerely) prepared to accept the same fate if the roles were reversed. A harsh creditor may be convinced that he too would deserve prison, whatever the consequences to himself or his family, if unable to pay his debt.[14] On Hare's grounds, however, the oppressive creditor is morally entitled to be (others may say immorally) oppressive provided his oppressiveness is consistent, for acting consistently he apparently also acts 'on principle', in conformity with the logical meaning of the word 'ought'; except of course that this is not a general principle but one personal or peculiar to himself. Not that Hare accepts this outcome unflinchingly; he rather hopes that his moral eccentric or fanatic will remain the rarest sort of bird. Whether or not this is a realistic expectation, it is not really to the point. Not only are there enough cruel persons in the world; so long as we can think of the mere possibility of oppressive actions occurring we need a moral basis for judging or condemning such acts: we need rational grounds for saying that such acts are wrong. At the very least, therefore, Hare's concessions to the fanatic undermine the very applicability of a moral theory just at one of the crucial points where we do need a moral principle by which to judge. Nor can his fanatic be severed from the rest of his theory, since Hare is almost inevitably led to his concessions by his belief that all moral arguments are *ad hominem*.[15]

THE CATEGORICAL IMPERATIVE

Kant dismissed the familiar golden rule argument, which he called 'the trivial *quod tibi non vis fieri etc.*'[16] He rightly saw that this argument cannot furnish a principle or universal law, yet his own substitute or improvement, known as the moral law or the categorical imperative, can be shown to suffer from other flaws which are worth being attended to. Kant, as everyone knows, distinguished between a categorical and a hypothetical imperative, the latter of which says that 'I ought to do something because I will something else', whereas the categorical imperative asserts: 'I ought to will thus or thus, whether or not I have willed something else'. While the hypothetical imperative is thus a 'precept of prudence' which we can always escape if we abandon our purpose, the categorical imperative states what ought to be done, whether it suits or pleases us or not. How, then, does the categorical imperative state this moral law? In its first and perhaps most fundamental formulation it does so simply by saying: 'act only on that maxim which you can at the same time will should become a universal law'.[17]

Now to the extent that this formulation points to a requirement of universalisability, or is merely another way of saying that we cannot reason morally except on the basis of general rules, the categorical imperative certainly expresses a most important condition, as we shall see further in Chapter 3. But the categorical imperative is meant to do considerably more than this: to serve as a canon of moral judgment, as a moral touchstone or criterion of what it is to act rightly or wrongly. For this purpose Kant advances two grounds why our actions must be 'willable' as a universal law, a narrower and a wider ground. The narrower suggests that some actions cannot even be conceived as universal laws as they cannot be universalised as maxims of actions without self-contradiction: so if everybody lied, there would be no truth; if everybody stole, there would be nothing left to be stolen; and if everybody made false promises, this would make promising itself impossible; no one would believe he was being promised anything as he would regard promises as empty shams.[18] However, there is a crucial weakness in this claim. The thief (to take him now as our principal example) may object that he too agrees that if everybody stole there would be no property, that this is in fact the last thing he wants, wishing on the contrary to uphold a respect for property, including a need for honesty among thieves. What, he may go on, distinguishes his case from others is that he and his fellow-thieves have special needs, and that in any case thieves constitute (or would wish to constitute) a small minority of citizens who cannot really threaten the institution of property as this is the sort of social institution which, to function effectively, requires only normal or frequent but by no means universal observance. Again, the thief may say that even if he is selfish in taking advantage of others, this is an entirely rational thing for him to do, given his own purposes, so that far from contradicting his will, what he does rather fulfils it. Hence, if selfishness can be rational, nothing has been shown why selfish actions cannot be willed.

Take next Kant's wider ground which, instead of the 'inner impossibility' of doing certain things (stealing, false promises etc.), rather concentrates on the impossibility to *will* to do certain things since so to will would be self-contradictory. It would be a contradiction for me to will not to help anyone in distress, for I cannot will this for my own case since I cannot will that I would never want help of any kind, even help when drowning, starving and so on. Though, at first sight this seems more powerful than the former ground, its flaw is that it does seem to confuse actual or immediate with purely hypothetical or more remote situations of help. For I may still be perfectly rational in abstractly wanting help, yet in concretely preferring not to incur the immediate inconvenience or disadvantage of having here and now to help others; also I may discount the possibility of my ever wanting the sort of help for which another is now asking; I may propose to make sure that the possibility will never arise or at least confidently expect that it never will: drowning or starving are, after all, not everybody's fact of life. It is true that I am most unkind in refusing help to another in distress, especially where such help would require little on my part, but this merely shows that I am unkind, not that I cannot will to be so. It follows that the alleged 'duty' to help others does not now arise from a requirement of reason, that of saving my will from nurturing a self-contradiction; rather it arises, if at all, from a purely prudential consideration, in that by helping others I may secure a sort of I.O.U. either from the person I am immediately helping, or from all other persons who may one day be able, even if possibly not always willing, to help me.

There remain one or two other objections to the categorical imperative. If it is, as Kant wanted it, to be seen as a universal law of nature, it can lead to an absurd absolutism or rigorism. Kant insisted that it can *never* be right to tell a lie, even if its effect would be thoroughly beneficent such as a lie to save a friend from mental, possibly fatal, shock, or a lie designed to mislead a maniac chasing another person (perhaps my friend) only to kill him. It has often been pointed out that to tell a lie in such circumstances would not be self-contradictory or self-defeating; it would be self-defeating only if a lie were a predictably useless manoeuvre to adopt. This points to a deeper inconsistency in Kant's theory. On the one hand, his theory requires (on its 'narrow' ground) a 'universal law' against lying so as not to create an 'inner impossibility' in our human practice of truth-telling. On the other hand, we are told (by the 'wider' ground) that we cannot will, save at the cost of self-contradiction, to refuse urgent help to others, help which surely must sometimes include help by telling a lie.[19]

Another difficulty of the categorical imperative has to do with the fact that there are actions that cannot be regarded as wrong, although, if universalised, they also lead to an 'inner impossibility' or contradiction. Take Brentano's well-known example of an imperative: 'do not accept (let everyone refuse) bribes'. Just as universal stealing would lead to the destruction of stealable things, so a universal refusal of bribes would lead to their extinction. On Kant's moral canon this could only be wrong, since this does not distinguish between theft and bribes; in fact it cannot even accommodate such a distinction. Can one then save Kant's theory with the help of another suggestion advanced by Singer, namely, that the purpose of all of us refusing bribes would be completely achieved, not defeated, as it would bring about the extinction of bribery, a far from undesirable result, hence something we have no reason not to will to become a universal law.[20] This suggestion however is distinctly odd. For in order to make it at all convincing, Singer has, he admits, to suppose that in refusing bribes we do so 'on moral grounds' because we regard bribery as wrong; to suppose this, moreover, 'is absolutely essential', for 'it is only on some such assumption as this that the consequence taken for granted in this objection can even plausibly be supposed to follow'.[21] Yet if so, what work is left for the categorical imperative? Are we not already assuming to be wrong what the moral imperative is supposed to tell us to be wrong? It therefore seems that far from Brentano being mistaken, his *reductio ad absurdum* must stand; though, to make this clear, it stands only to defeat the categorical imperative as a comprehensive or sufficient canon of moral judgement; it does not affect the requirement of universalisability which the canon also contains.

Of course the categorical imperative could be rewritten in terms of universalisability, that is, as the principle that we must judge actions in terms of general rules, the vital importance of which Kant certainly fully recognised. 'The essence of morality', he insisted, 'is that our actions are motivated by a general rule, that is, that the reasons for the action are to be found in such a general rule'.[22] What it seems Kant did not fully appreciate is that reason, as it aids and furthers analysis, can indeed reveal formal conditions or requirements, but cannot also function cognitively as an immediate or direct source of practical moral rules. If reason did so function we would in fact no longer need moral rules, nor for that matter moral theories, for we would then be able to 'deduce', or to work out, what we have to do in each case.

The true sources of morality lie in the facts of social life, in our inter-personal grievances about what is done or what is due to us. And all that reason can do is to help us argue about these grievances more confidently or systematically.

PERSONAL COMMITMENTS AND MORAL JUDGEMENTS

From all we have said it should then be evident that morality is not just a matter of oneself making a moral decision, or personally committing oneself to a moral act, of prescribing to oneself a moral view, nor just a matter of personal sincerity and personal moral strength. It is pre-eminently a matter of being able to assess or judge somebody's action morally, that is, in terms of moral rules. If moral judgements were really self-prescriptive or self-commanding, as some moral theories strongly suggest, then moral fanaticism or its opposite, moral weakness, would make morality as irrelevant as it would be inoperative.

Indeed moral weaknesses or indifference must be the starting-point of any moral theory, in the sense that they are the major human obstacles that a moral theory has to overcome. We would not need moral rules were we not morally 'unholy' or eccentric or morally weak; we may often be kindly enough, but then often we are not; nor can we rely on our mutual good will or good intentions, for with these the road to hell is paved. Hence we need moral rules by which we can (no longer autonomously or personally but now heteronomously or, as it were, supra-personally) justify or judge our actions and, ..iore particularly, those actions giving rise to complaints or grievances; and we need rules informed by arguable reasons, not simply action-ordering imperatives.

Not that our self-prescriptions, our personal moral beliefs or judgements, are unimportant things. To recognise their existence such as they are certainly helps to account for the complexly felt emotions known as moral conscience. To say, for example, 'I ought not to have hurt him but couldn't help myself', shows that the 'ought' retains enough prescriptive force to cause remorse or a sense of guilt, based on an awareness that I 'failed' to do what I ought to have done. Hare rightly insists that 'prescriptive uses of moral language exist', and that, concomitantly, statements or remorse or guilt presume the remnants of a sense of duty, otherwise remorse or guilty conscience could not really arise.[23] Such views of moral language offer significant and sharp insights into our moral psychology. But valuable though they are, they have no direct relevance for present purposes. Our purpose now is not with moral psychology but with moral reasoning, with a rational basis for the moral judgeability of certain human actions and ends, including their rightness or wrongness. From this point of view it matters little whether a human agent is weak yet sincere; the fact that we believe a person to be sincere may certainly increase the 'truth-value', so to speak, of his kindly protestations as one can more readily expect kindness from somebody who has shown sincere affection before; even so, a man can act rightly however insincere, just as he can act wrongly sincere though he may be. Similarly it now matters little whether a person is remorseful or conscience-stricken after the event, or is throughout morally indifferent or ignorant or is a fanatic. Even with regard to the latter, and especially him, we—the rest of us—do not withhold moral judgement. Just as a person who fails to take prudential advice can still be said to act imprudently, so a person who fails to act according to moral advice or to a moral rule can be judged to act immorally.

3 A Calculus of Avoidable Harm

The present chapter will take a more constructive turn, the intention being to show how rational moral argument can proceed, and what its rational foundations are. Not that one can offer a rational model for all moral disputes: these are too many and various, in fact as manifold and variable as our feelings and passions or our social ideas and ideals are. Still one can construct a rational model for one or two basic and large departments of inter-personal grievances, in particular those arising from avoidable harm, the physical or other harm done by one person to another. It is in this area, perhaps principally in this, that we can identify, and put to work, two conditions of moral thinking, two related conditions which together make up our rational model, one of which is a purely formal condition, known as universalisability; the other a more substantive condition which, for lack of a better word, we may call harm-oriented normativity. The former condition has to do with a necessary element in any moral rule as a *rule*, the latter with the content or direction of that rule, the sort of action the rule is concerned to prescribe or proscribe. Not that the presence of these conditions proves the existence of morality, only the logical requirements we have to fulfil for a statement to qualify as a moral one. We are, in short, concerned with indirect, or logical, proof that unpacks the assumptions of certain discourse, not with direct or empirical proof that something is the case.

It will now have become plain that what we mean by moral argument or moral reasoning is an argument depending on rules by which we can judge (judge 'objectively', so to speak) a person's actual or contemplated actions in relation to another person. A person doing what he does to another thus exposes himself to being judged according to rules; he will have to justify his action either by showing the particular grievance or complaint against him to be morally unfounded or by offering some valid excuse. For, as we have also seen, we cannot just give any reasons for our actions, such as reasons that explain what we do in terms of our own personal desires or preferences, however kindly or benevolent these may be; we have to give what are in the nature of 'external' or 'objective' reasons, that is, reasons which not only can serve as common standards to which we can appeal over and above our personal attitudes, but can also be reasons which make the argument relatively concludable in that an action can be judged as being either right or wrong. Indeed without such a relative concludability, moral reasoning would not be very significant; it would be an exchange of words rather than exchange of arguments: the two sides would be either issuing orders at each other, or comparing emotive notes, or shouting at each other, or trying to persuade each other in the way advertisers do.

A rational model of moral argument is no less important for the purposes of law or legal reasoning. Take a judge who is to decide for or against a party who has suffered injury; suppose there is neither a statute nor a precedent for him to fall back on, thus no positive legal source or precept to guide his decision either way; suppose further that the judge cannot refuse to decide, nor can decide, at least not openly so, according to his own personal discretion. It is obvious that the judge cannot arrive at what could be called a 'just' decision unless he adopts forms of reasoning that apply moral rules; unless, more particularly, he follows a model of reasoning that is informed by criteria by which a particular judgement can be supported as a morally right one, or at least as one not palpably wrong. Also, where a judge so judges, he will act very much in the tradition of natural law; not in the sense in which natural law has been, sometimes still is, taken to constitute a sort of silent yet somehow superior source of law capable of overriding even operative or positive law, such as an established statute; in which sense, indeed, natural law rests on a fallacy as it becomes virtually self-contradictory to speak of a law as unjust or immoral, since, under the natural-legal dispensation, such a law would at once collapse. We are using 'natural law' in a more modest sense according to which a judge not only may but must arrive at moral decisions on rational grounds, wherever there is a gap in the law which it is for the judge to fill.

In this sense, furthermore, legal naturalism can in fact co-exist with legal positivism, since this version of natural law gives positive law its superior (political) head, at any rate so far as the positive rules will go; it only denies that positivism can explain, or in fact was meant to explain, the characteristic activity of a judge or judging where positivism no longer applies. Naturalism then takes judging to be something essentially different from legislating or commanding or merely exercising a discretion as officials do; judging rather becomes a form of reasoning which has to justify its results or conclusions. To judge an action as right or wrong the judgement can no longer resort to superior authority or rely on a superior text (for this merely throws us back to positivism), but will have to be supported on independent grounds. A legal naturalism of this sort even retrieves, as we shall later see, the old-fashioned distinction between *mala prohibita* and *mala in se*; we now need precisely some such doctrine as *mala in se* since without it we cannot explain the characteristic role of a judge. Whereas a legislator can, by virtue merely of his political authority, establish *mala prohibita* (this is, in fact, what the phrase means), a judge, in the strict non-legislative role in which we now see him, has no such political power: his function is to decide or determine a dispute or grievance on the basis, not so much of imposed, as of perennial or 'natural' rights and wrongs; 'natural' because backed by demonstrably rational criteria which are far removed from political change. What we are saying about judges and judging in fact applies to everybody concerned to provide rational or 'objective' reasons for a moral view. For, as the 'ideal observer' theory has partly seen, we cannot conduct a rational moral argument unless we look at a particular problem rather as judges do, whether in doing so we are judging a personal complaint, or a case involving other persons or are simply trying to argue rationally about a moral problem we wish to resolve.

REASONS, RULES AND UNIVERSALISABILITY

For a reason for action to form or become part of a standard or rule, that reason must be generalisable or universalisable not so much in order to encompass a universality of instances as, rather, to make it apply not, as normal imperatives do, to particular or listable persons commanded to do or not to do certain things, but to actions of a specified description, of a stated kind or class. So where A advances a grievance against B, as where A complains that he has been harmed by B, the grounds or reasons for that grievance have to be universalised to enable both sides to argue as equals, one with the other; for unless they so do they would not be sharing a reason or rule in respect of the harmful action; either side would simply give *his* (personal) reason, A for complaining as he does, B for his action, at best merely explaining why he did what he did. Both A and B, in other words, would not be giving a reason capable of justifying or excusing the complaint, they would instead be withholding the common reason or standard on the basis of which alone a rational argument can unfold. To argue together the two sides have so to depersonalise or universalise their reasons not only to ensure that neither side can make superior claims, but by the same token to lead them to argue about the 'merits' of the case.

This does not mean that the two sides are precluded from referring to their human or personal wants (or their individual desires or interests), if only because one's grievances very much derive from wants. What universalisation does mean is that we cannot make claims except on the basis of these wants being also common or shared wants; the two sides cannot argue as equals unless they assume a mutual equality of at least certain wants or interests. This is not to suggest that men do have equal or identical wants, for plainly they do not. The point, rather, is that for A and B to argue as equals about wants, an initial (logical) requirement is that they must recognise as between each other the existence of similar *kinds* of wants (or desires or interests), that is, kinds of wants that may nevertheless allow for some differences of degree. If either A or B could advance his purely personal or idiosyncratic wishes or wants as a reason, or if (what comes to the same thing) either could say that his wants are 'special' or 'exceptional', then they would be unable even to start an argument, moral reasoning between them would never get off the ground. This is so even where A and B are arguing about what appear like very special or very personal interests or wants; because here, too, they will need to argue in terms of a kind or class of claims, however much the particular claim may constitute one member of a class. For a one-member class must be sharply differentiated from the so-called unique situations so dear to existentialists; a unique situation by its very nature excludes comparable instances and thus excludes rules, whereas a one-member class does not exclude comparable instances: the one member of the class is fortuitously but not necessarily unique.

Going a step further, we may even say that merely by dint of arguing about equal kinds of wants, A and B are led to recognise equal *rights* between themselves. For an important feature of the word 'right' is that it refers to precisely such common and equally claimable wants, wants that are thus attuned to a standard as well as incorporated in a rule. Unless wants are standardised we could not even know, when one person says he has a right against another, in respect of what interchangeable wants a right is claimed; and unless the right is part of a rule, there would be no claim or demand even suggesting that we must somehow give effect to that right. A right, it may now become clearer, is then not just a claim or demand, it is (as some legal theorists have at least partly seen) more in the nature of a 'protected interest': that is, the interest is based on a kind or class of wants or interests which, in principle, anyone may claim, while the protection comes from the demand being backed by a heteronomous rule either of a moral sort or one that, by acquiring a coercive dimension, turns into a legal rule.

This heteronomous element also explains why in judging the grievance we have to look at it not alone from the point of view of A's complaint, but no less from the side of B; for the part of the rule containing the action-guiding 'ought' is directed to B as it is B's actions that have to be guided if the purpose is to protect A's rights. This is why moral or, for that matter, legal rules usually fasten on actions, the rule rather concentrating on what a duty-bearer should or should not do.[1] Of course these actions, too, have to be depersonalised or universalised to function as moral rules. Instead of saying 'you (A) must not do this (X) to B', we have to exclude A and B confining ourselves to X, such as 'one must not (or ought not to) do X' or 'one must not do X in situation Y'. The point of universalising is the same as before. Just as we need to create equal rights between A and B, since only such equal rights can apply to all similar persons, so the correlative duties we impose must be 'universally' applicable as well; what is prescribed as right or wrong for one person must be right or wrong for any similar person, that is, any person doing the same or similar acts. We begin to see that wherever we have rule-governed conduct rights and duties come in pairs, the rights indicating the source of our grievances, emanating from our desires or wants, the duties specifying the actions, usually the negative actions or forbearances, that safeguard our wants and keep them inviolate.

Universalisability thus operates to furnish anonymous rules that contain general rights and duties which, though they may originate in a particular grievance by A against B, yet are universal to this extent that they are potentially applicable to all members of a class, the X-doing as well as X-suffering class. It is a class which logicians call an 'intensional' as distinct from an 'enumerative' class, a distinction which reflects the broader requirement that a moral rule has to apply to an unforeseen and indefinite number of cases, so that it has to be addressed to *anybody*, not *everybody*, in a class. Since 'everybody' cannot now be listed in advance, since a moral rule does not in any case address itself to listed or named persons like an imperative, the purpose of universalisability becomes essentially this: to have the rule define itself in terms of actions or equal wants, these being the very terms of the moral argument. All of this shows again the intimate connection between morality and rationality, just as it shows how universalisability puts the rational arguer very much in the position of a judge, virtually of any judge whether he be a judge at a cat-show or in a court of law. For a judge, though he may have personal views about a thing or act, has to judge, and as a judge, declare himself in terms of rules, he cannot just state his own preferences as they affect either of two sides; if he did he would not judge but rather dictate his views. Nor should this requirement be confused with the more familiar judicial requirement of impartiality; universalisability goes deeper because it represents a logical constituent or condition in the *formation* as distinct from the *application* of a rule. So whereas impartiality is required to keep (or to work according to) a rule, universalisability is required to make a rule: it forms part of the very concept of a rule.

There remain one or two misconceptions about universalisability we may briefly advert to as this may throw further light on some features of moral reasoning. One misconception is that universalisability is simply akin to logical consistency. Just as saying 'this is red' commits one to the proposition that anything like this would likewise have to be red, so moral judgements (it is contended) have to be consistent in the same way: hence if 'this (X) is good' everything like X must, speaking consistently, also be good.[2] However colour and moral statements are not quite so comparable as these examples imply. To say 'this A is red' is certainly inconsistent with 'this A is not red'; to say both of A would be misusing language precisely because it would be self-contradictory. Similarly you cannot say 'I want X' and 'I don't want X' in the same breath, or in quick succession, for to say both would merely cancel what you assert while asserting it. But the important point is that in the latter case you can change your mind: you can say 'I want X' and then, after due reflection, 'No, I don't want X', without there being any contradiction at all. Moreover, you can change your mind in a way you cannot do in respect of 'this is red', simply because in relation to colour- (or other object-) words you cannot, unilaterally, change the rules as to which objects are to be called red, these being rules of language which do not depend on you alone, whereas in 'I want X' you are not so committed since it is precisely the function of 'I want X' to allow you to change your mind unilaterally. The same however is not true where instead of 'I want (to do) X' you say 'I ought to want (or do) X' where the 'ought' is used not simply as a piece of self-admonition but as part of a rule; for the point of using the latter 'ought' is to recognise that one's freedom is now restricted, that one can no longer change one's mind. It follows that universalisability is then not like consistency, but is rather an essential condition of rules, rules that are meant to guide our conduct quite irrespective of what we ourselves may, from time to time, be minded to do. This is precisely why Kant took moral rules to be moral laws.

A second misconception is that prudential reasons, being practical reasons, are as universalisable as moral reasons. Yet prudential rules differ crucially from moral ones. In the latter, as we have just seen, we require universalisability to convert moral reasons into rules that do restrict, or purport to restrict, our personal freedom to change our minds, whereas in the case of prudential rules universality arises naturally and intrinsically. For to say 'I ought to do X', where the ought is a prudential one, is to speak of the 'right' or the 'better' means to an end, necessary means as they derive from the empirical or scientific knowledge we have or accept; it is this knowledge which is 'universal', being knowledge of the external world. Prudential reasons thus refer to means, not to ends, for these ends one may always change—a freedom completely absent in the moral case where the whole emphasis is on ends, the universalisable point being precisely to withdraw these ends from free personal choice.

UNIVERSALISABILITY NOT A SUFFICIENT CONDITION

Important as universalisability is, it is still not enough for the formation of moral rules, being only a first step, a necessary but still not a sufficient one. For, obviously, it is not enough to say that moral argument requires rules; we must go further to indicate, even if only in outline, what the rules are to be about: what sort of human actions, reciprocal commissions or omissions, moral rules are to comprise. Universalisability, in other words, only gives us a formal or second-order rule, while the practical rule we now need must in guiding our actions also make contact with the human conduct it is supposed to guide. Without this practical, action-specific, element we shall later describe as normativity, our moral rule would simply not do its job; it would remain not merely purely formal but vacuously formal, without even a hint as to what its content, let alone its moral content, might be. Indeed all formal principles must sooner or later connect with substantive phenomena, for unless they do they have nothing to be formal about. Formal principles are parasitic on, logical auxiliaries for, matters of substance, not substitutes for them.

A substantive element is no less essential to distinguish moral from other rules, especially rules based on non-moral value-judgements, since non-moral value-judgements, too, are universalisable. So where a judge at a cat-show judges cat A to be a 'first-class' specimen, he will have to judge any other cat that possesses the same qualities in the same way. As a judge he is not entitled to change his views as between cats substantially alike, for judging means deciding according to rules, though we still have not said what *sort* of rules; for unless we say what sort of rules, in a substantive rather than purely logical sense, the whole formal enterprise of saying that the judge must act justly or impartially, or according to rules, would not be worth saying, the rule would have, normatively, nothing to fasten on. To be operative the rules would therefore have to specify some of the prized features of cats: features, for example, possessed by well-bred but not free-roaming types. Yet whatever the relevant rules here might be, their substance would not allow us to describe them as moral rules—why not we shall shortly see.

What is more, without a substantive component we would not even be able to identify the like cases that are to be treated alike. For how are we to distinguish between like and unlike situations, or between legitimate differences and illegitimate ones, or (more broadly) between similarities and differences that are relevant from case to case? Suppose (to return to an example of Hare's) that a defaulting debtor should not go to prison if his skin is white, but that he should if he happens to be black. The white-black distinction seems at first sight to include an easily universalisable test, one between so to speak, like (white) and unlike (black) debtors; but though formally impeccable, as a moral distinction it turns out to be as irrelevant as it is unacceptable: we cannot, it will be agreed, decide morally to send people to prison merely because of the colour of their skin. Hare arrives at the same conclusion by saying that a morally relevant property has to be universal, one describable without reference to individuals, for only a universal property can apply to all persons alike; so if the property is not universal, we do not meet 'the demand for universalisability, and cannot claim to be putting forward a moral argument at all'.[3] But to say this, is neither wholly true nor really enough. Not true, because a white-black distinction does not, by itself, defy the demand for universalisability: we can have a rule, having made a (universalisable) value-judgement, under which only white, but not black, cats qualify for the first prize. Not enough, because to speak of a universal property is merely another way of restating the need for a general rule. Without such a rule our argument would consist of a verbal exchange of commands or preferences but would not lead to a genuine argument; though even then we are as yet still not really saying what the argument, and especially a moral argument, is to be about: that, in particular, it is to be about conduct as well as conduct of a certain kind. Of course where an argument, instead of having first to construct rules, can already assume their existence, as is of course the case where we talk or argue about existing moral or legal rules, we do not need to resort to or to seek out the formal condition of universalisability precisely because in such moral (or legal) discourse the demand for universalisability is already met.

To insist that universalisability is only a formal principle is by no means to suggest that it is a trivial one, as Broad and Bradley maintained, on the ground that it does not say very much, being a 'bare tautology'.[4] Their criticism rightly points out that one can always identify various similarities or differences between cases without indicating what the relevant moral similarities or differences are. Still this criticism only shows that universalisability is a necessary condition, not also a sufficient one. Nor is this insufficiency really cured by Singer's wider thesis or by what he calls the generalisation argument, according to which the function of universalisability or of the generalisation principle is not to determine relevant similarities or differences between situations, but merely to indicate the logical need for generality, so that the expression 'similar persons in similar circumstances' has to be seen as a 'place holder' or as 'blanks' to be filled in in different contexts.[5] To be sure, Singer does concede that without showing how these blanks can be filled in the generalisation argument would not work; accordingly he offers some criteria for determining what in certain contexts would be relevantly similar or different. Unfortunately Singer does not seem really successful just in this respect, for all he can finally show is substantially only this: that just as an act adjudged right for one person must be equally right for a class of persons, so the criteria for all similar or different cases are contained in the grounds or reasons on the strength of which an act is, or can be said to be, right or wrong. This, however, is not of great help. Not only is the formal point already conceded, namely that cases cannot be described as different or similar unless they belong to the same general class, but Bradley's criticism does not, or at any rate need not, deny that a reason or ground for holding an action similar or different must be one specifying a relevant similarity or difference. What we still do not know is what it is that makes two actions *relevantly* like or unlike— 'relevantly' from a distinctly moral point of view. In the end, therefore, Singer seems to do little more than restate the formal requirement he started from: that a rational argument requires general reasons simply because general reasons allow for general rules. [6] In the end, in short, universalisability, while close to generality, is still not quite the same as it. In discourse involving value-judgements universalisability is necessary precisely to ensure generality; it is, so to speak, a 'disciplining' condition, required to make sure that the reasons we do give *are* general. But universalisability does not do more than this.

NORMATIVITY: THE EMERGENCE OF NORMS

Though it may now be clearer that universalisability alone is not enough, and that moral rules cannot operate without at least some indication of what these rules are to be about, how do we go about establishing the substance of moral rules, how can we say what their typical action-guiding content is to be? What is more, we do not start out with some formal principle of universalisability always in attendance, only waiting to be fleshed out with appropriate moral acts or events. Our 'original position', or what we shall now take to be our original position, rather is that we start with inter-personal grievances, with acts or facts about which we complain, yet grievances we want to argue about rather than take matters into our own hands. Clearly the first task is to make these complaints or grievances intelligible to ourselves and to others, to regiment these grievances as arguments and, accordingly, to identify and assemble the reasons on which they are based. To do this, as we shall now see, we must accept or assume the existence of certain norms, certain regular expectations between persons about their behaviour between themselves or in a group which, still speaking very broadly, we shall soon realise to be, often and typically, norms or expectations concerned with the infliction of harm or hurt.

How, then, do such harm-oriented norms come to exist or emerge? Consider, to begin with, a very simple example which will illustrate the basic structure of a normative relationship. Suppose that in a private situation such as between husband and wife, the wife has come to expect her husband to behave regularly in certain respects, e.g. to come home at certain times, while for his part the husband has become aware of, and virtually accepts, the wife's expec-tations. Any irregular behaviour by him may cause disap-pointment to the wife, let us say significant disappointment if only because her regular expectations remain importantly unfulfilled. The husband, too, knowing that his wife expects him to behave in a certain (regular) way, will know what she is talking about should she voice a complaint, while to lessen her disappointment he might even advance some excuse. It is this mutual expectation about a certain type of behaviour we now call a 'norm', meaning by that word not what it usually means, namely, a prescriptive rule, whether a moral or legal rule, but meaning rather a standard of judging or valuing certain acts in the light of regular or 'normal' or normally expectable conduct; although, as in this case, the norm represents as yet only a very private or restricted standard obtaining between two individuals alone. Still it is important to see that *mutual* expectations are of the very essence of such a norm, for it is this 'complementarity of expectations' that distinguishes such expectations from others we may have about other social events, such as expecting the weather to change or expecting a train to arrive on time.[7]

Without this complementarity the husband would not know how to make choices concerning his own behaviour, how to do what is right rather than wrong, for to make a right or a wrong choice implies that he can relate action to the more or less predictable reaction of the other person concerned, here his wife; nor, additionally, would he know what it means to 'disappoint' his wife, nor would the wife have anything to complain about. Without mutual expectations, again, a person would not know how to behave responsibly, simply because what we call responsible action means that a person is not just living, like a child, from moment to moment, however 'regular' (because habit-like) these moments may sequentially appear, but is acting within a normative context of particular or possible obligations and excuses, precisely the context which allows him to act with the foresight and awareness of the possible effects of his actions, including the grievances or complaints he might be expected to meet. Without mutual expectations, in short, it would in fact be utterly immaterial whether the husband acted regularly or not; his regularity or otherwise would be an accident of nature, it could never give rise to any norm between himself and his wife.

It follows that to talk intelligibly about their mutual obligations or excuses, to say that the wife has a grievance or that the husband is somehow answerable to her, husband and wife must share a common standard or norm, there must be (as Wittgenstein put it, though admittedly not quite in the

same context) 'agreement not only in definitions but also
(queer as it may seem) in judgements'.[8] But in what way
must their judgments agree? Clearly they do not merely
agree regarding the fact that theirs has been a regular
relationship; surely their agreement would now have to
include (what we may call) 'warm' rather than 'cold'
knowledge as to what, between each other, it means or feels
like to have a disappointment or the mental or 'spiritual' pain
or discomfort associated with it. The husband may still say
that his being irregular (late for dinner) is too minor a hurt to
be worth talking about, or that he does not wish to talk about
it at all, in which latter case no argument would be possible.
However if he does join issue with the wife, he will have to
judge the hurt or disappointment he has caused in the same
way as the wife does; accordingly he may respond by
offering some excuse such as that the train was late or that he
was detained in his work etc., that is, offer excuses which
would disclaim or deny his own responsibility in causing his
wife's pain. The present 'agreement in judgements' then
consists of two parts: the two sides must agree, or by their
verbal conduct may be taken to agree, as to what it is that
may cause them disappointment or pain; and they further
agree that, as far as they can, they will not act in relation to
each other so as to cause any physical or mental harm. In
other words, it is the reality or possibility of deliberate or
avoidable harm that becomes the moral standard by which
they judge their behaviour between themselves.

Such a moral standard, needless to say, is entirely different
from (for example) a metric standard which is principally
designed to help us measure things more conveniently as well
as uniformly; a moral standard rather purports to indicate a
class of acts or events that is to form the substantive
component of a moral rule, thus also to enable us to distinguish more distinctly between moral value-judgements
and non-moral ones. It follows that such a standard robs the
moral rule of its neutrality just as it makes moral rules very
different from the rules of games. The latter, we see again,

merely specify the means according to which a certain contest can take place, though we remain free to play the game or not. Moral rules, on the other hand, are rules about ends, their purpose being precisely the non-neutral one of thwarting our freedom wherever that freedom threatens to go in the direction of harm.

What we have said about private norms applies in a more complex way to (the emergence of) public or social norms, i.e. norms not just shared by two specific individuals in a specific relationship but shared by all members in a group. Yet the immediate question now is: how can a complementarity of expectations arise here? The broad answer is that, in a group, complementary expectations must be anchored in a wide (multilateral) social experience, not just in one (restricted) course of conduct, as it can in a private (bilateral) relationship: they are, in other words, multilateral expectations about inter-personal conduct that human beings would share by dint merely of living in a group or community. To take a concrete example, consider the familiar but fundamental case of A doing some physical injury to B. Under what circumstances can we say that B has a justified complaint or that A has done a 'wrong', i.e. has breached a standard of conduct represented by a norm? It will be plain that unless we can assume that B has come to expect his 'regular' or 'normal' immunity from such injury, his complaint or critical reaction against A's act can make little or no sense, the more so since A would himself have no reason to expect B's critical reaction to the harm done. Let us be clear, however, what this critical reaction involves. It is not merely that B is angered by the pain inflicted on him and in revenge reacts similarly against A; for this could be a purely instinctive or impulsive reaction instead of being also a reflective or critical one. No doubt angry or violent reactions are significant enough events in our social world: 'don't make him angry', 'don't provoke him' can be very useful bits of advice that A might well heed before doing anything against B. Nevertheless A's knowledge of B's possible anger only gives him some knowledge of certain facts about B. It does not, in particular, yield standards of behaviour; without shared or mutual expectations it would make no sense for B to complain of or to criticise A's act; it would make no sense precisely because any *justified* complaint or criticism requires referability to some shared standard or norm. When a German jurist, Jellinek, referred in a famous phrase to the 'normative force of the factual' ('die normative Kraft des Faktischen'), his normative net was cast too wide; for not all so-called social facts are norm-creative, only those involving mutual expectations are.

But, to return to our A–B example, how can a norm or standard emerge in this case? What are here the mutual expectations that would allow us to regard A's action as a deviation from a norm? Unlike our previous husband-and-wife example where the wife's expectations built on the husband's regular behaviour, the present situation has no such background of regular acts. Still, this lack of regularity is more apparent than real, provided we realise that regular expectations may result not only from positive but also from negative acts, from regular omissions or forbearances. As between A and B, and other persons like them in the same group, we must be able to presuppose a state of affairs that takes at least this for granted, namely, a normal, even if not invariable, immunity from at least intentional physical harm; we must be able to presuppose that, as an ordinary condition of their daily life, members of a group can well expect it to be more 'normal' for them *not* to suffer rather than to suffer pain, that is, pain caused or inflicted by another member of the group as distinct from pain caused by sickness or misfortune or some other act of God. Unless indeed we can assume such an immune *status quo*, we could not even say that the members of the group enjoy peaceable social relationships, or possess a sort of basic sociability, however imperfect or unstable that sociability may be. Such a sociable assumption, to mention this but in passing, runs counter to the well-known Hobbesian hypothesis of an original war of all against all. While we can accept a hypothetical war by some against some, or even many against some, what seems impossible to accept is a situation of each fighting each since this would exclude any other expectation than pain or harm, a situation that would allow no room for harm-avoiding norms or standards to evolve; with maniac fighting maniac there would be no opportunity of learning what it is to have non-hostile expectations creative of shared standards or norms or, indeed, what it is to have non-violent relationships. Nor can we imagine that appropriate norms might nevertheless be introduced by our own enlightened self-interest or by a leviathan who may be tyrannically cruel only to be benevolently kind: all these enlightened or benevolent intentions would end in nothing unless there already existed some regular expectation or social norm of a reasonably regular immunity from harm.

Furthermore, to suppose such a sociable state of affairs implies that we start, and indeed must start, with a concomitant assumption of at least some degree of personal liberty; that is, with the assumption that human beings, though they may differ individually in their physical or intellectual capabilities or interests, are nevertheless equally expecting to be left alone, at any rate to the extent of remaining free to do or act as they are severally able and willing to act. Unless we make this assumption it makes little sense to assert personal rights, including rights against injury, for we cannot have any such rights unless we assume at least this right, for every person to be equally free, i.e. free from harm. This assumption thus reveals an important 'inner' connection between the ideas of liberty and harm. A grievance about harm presupposes one's right to be free, for what could a grievance or complaint be about otherwise; conversely, one's right to be free would not be worth stating if it did not, first and foremost, give one grounds to complain against avoidable harm. In this sense the notion of liberty not only connects with that of one's (harm-less) immunity, it concomitantly imposes limits upon the freedom of human action, these limits now being precisely those that make for the avoidance of the sort of harm necessarily resulting from the collisions in human conduct if everyone pursued, completely freely, his own ends or interests.

So seen, liberty, immunity and harm rather specify the basic conditions under which our personal ends can be at least co-existable or compatible. They are conditions, it is true, which do not make our ends also mutually happy or harmonious, but this is not now the object of the exercise, that object being simply to prevent harm, not to establish a euphoric consensus in a group. Kant saw this very clearly: justice, he maintained, is the aggregate of those conditions under which the freedom of one person, including his freedom of will or action, can co-exist with the freedom of everyone under a universal law or general principle.[9]

SOCIAL ASSUMPTIONS AND MORAL RULES

Still what does it mean to say that a group 'shares' a moral norm, or that a group 'has', or that 'we' have, a moral standard or, if one prefers, a sort of tacit social agreement against the infliction of harm? To answer this very broadly, we can say that a standard arises, to begin with, from a sort of *vicarious* sharing of certain emotive attitudes by the group as a whole, or at least a substantial part thereof. Thus Strawson helpfully distinguishes between personal and vicarious re-sentments, the latter mainly arising on behalf of others, without one's own interest or dignity being involved; indeed, an attitude or reaction is not a moral one unless *capable* of being vicarious just in this sense.[10] It is such vicarious sharing that seems to underlie what some thinkers such as Dürkheim have seen as a sort of 'collective conscience', or what Hume described as the 'spark of friendship for human kind' or as our 'generous sentiments', or what Hare called the 'ingredient of sympathetic imagination', a sort of vicarious sympathy that makes us capable of caring about pain and suffering not just to ourselves but to others as well.[11] There are cases in which these vicarious feelings alone make or mobilise the social complaint: where a person is murdered, or a small child ill-treated, neither victim is usually in a position to voice his grievance for the harm done; hence without the vicarious resentment of the group, murder and child-battering would never be the operative moral wrongs they so plainly are. There are other cases in which the vicarious attitudes of the group may override a victim's willingness to forgive or forget. Though, as the well-known maxim 'volenti non fit injuria' partly indicates, one's moral right not to be harmed is a right one can waive or modify even to the point of abandoning one's privilege to complain, there are situations where just this is not countenanced: the criminal law, as everyone knows, does not generally entitle one to waive an injury; nor can one nowadays contract to suffer harm by, for example, selling oneself into slavery.

To point to these vicarious reactions is by no means to claim that a group is thereby endowed with a fund of precise values, with a ready code of specific moral rules. All we have is a social norm or presumption against the infliction of harm, and a norm which still only gives us a somewhat vague and indeterminate end. The norm is vague because our 'social' judgements concerning harm, including our collective resentments and disapprovals of injury, begin as and remain individual judgements, vicarious though they may also be. For in saying what it is, in certain actions, that we condemn as 'bad' or harmful for others, or in that sense 'bad' for everybody, each one of us starts only with the knowledge of what is bad or harmful for him. There is then in a group's total judgement as to what is a 'bad' action an initial and ineliminably individual component, even though our individual feelings or reactions must, both empirically and logically, still be (assumed to be) sufficiently coincident or convergent to allow these individual feelings to aggregate, vicariously yet concordantly, into something constituting the group's general moral standard or norm.[12] Still, as just

said, this convergence can never constitute an exact concor-
dance, for the social norm is not like a wall built of identical
bricks, of identical units of reactive or emotive attitudes.
They are not identical because our sensibilities to physical or
mental or economic harm differ from person to person, just
as harm to ourselves or to those near or dear to us weighs
more heavily with each of us than pain inflicted on persons
who are remote or hardly known. This, or something like
this, constitutes the important truth in the emotive theory of
morals which, whatever its broader intentions, has been right
to stress this personal dimension emerging from each
individual's own moral sentiments. What moral emotivism
has overlooked is that moral theory cannot stop here, since
we cannot (as earlier pointed out) judge people according to
our own likes and dislikes but have to judge on principle or
according to rules.

Again it is because our ultimate moral norm or standard is
and remains vague, often even inarticulate, that we have to
translate it into action-specific rules as and when concrete
grievances arise. The translated rule will conceptualise the
given kind of harm, anchoring it in the fact-situation that
gave rise to the complaint. This translation, moreover, will
somehow 'average out' or stabilise the notion of harm at least
for that situation, in that in conceptualising the harm the
latter now loses its personal 'intensivity'; for, being expressed
in more concrete or public language, the rule becomes, so to
speak, public property. As such, this and similar moral rules
become, as they are of course meant to be, the immediate
premises for further moral reasoning, to be followed or
qualified in other situations; the accumulating moral rules
also turn into a 'body' of knowledge which members of the
group can now be told or taught in advance or which can be
passed on to future generations. Indeed to say that a people
have a 'culture' is to say that, as well as sharing a common
language or common arts and crafts, they have a stock of
moral rules or values about at least some human actions or
some states of affairs.

The fact remains that for all their new action-specificity these rules must still assume (the existence of) a tacit, perhaps non-verbalised, but generally shared norm against the infliction of harm. For unless we can presume or presuppose such a norm our moral rules would simply not be intelligible as moral rules; we would not know what informs a moral rule, or how or to what purpose a moral rule could be established, or qualified, or how it could be regarded as similar to or different from another moral rule. In other words, without a harm-oriented norm or standard we would be unable to deal with new moral problems, or deal with new grievances, the catalogue of problems or grievances being never closed. Without a harm-oriented standard, moreover, we would in fact have no way of explaining how moral rules can arise, except to say that they arise fortuitously, or arise by the authority of some enlightened despot, though it can be seen that such explanations would, quite apart from being implausible, deprive the rules of their specifically moral content; they would not explain how moral rules can and do express a generally shared standard, one shared by all members of the group. Without assuming a shared interest against harm, we could therefore not even begin to explain the social energy or pressure or heteronomous force behind a moral rule, nor how in a group or society social criticism or reaction is awakened or mobilised against the breach of a rule; nor how harm or injury becomes an occasion for censure and condemnation instead of being left an insignificant or indifferent event, one to be taken notice of, if at all, by an omniscient sovereign but not by anyone else.

RESPONSIBLE ACTIONS AND COMPLAINABLE HARM

Moral rules, we then have argued, must have a special direction or import, in that they are rules incorporating prescriptions against specific human actions, actions having to do with the infliction of harm. It is also this concern with *avoidable* harm which, we shall now try to show, unifies a large part of the moral inquiry as to how we can and do judge actions and their resulting grievances. Thus an emphasis on avoidability leads directly to the basic distinction between avoidable and unavoidable, or inevitable, injury. If harm comes to you unavoidably, happening inevitably because of death or sickness, or earthquakes or floods, we could not resent, nor blame or condemn each other; we rather have to accept things as they happen to us, being things that cannot be made the subject of human action-rules. This, precisely, is one simple meaning of the aphorism that 'ought implies can': ought implies can because a rule about practical actions must address itself to a free or capable agent; it would be futile to address it to those who cannot help what they are or do: we cannot order the blind to see.

Again, to speak of avoidable injury is to direct immediate attention to the agent's motivation, to what lawyers call the 'intention' or 'mental element' with which an act is done. A deliberate act is clearly the most amenable action to be formulated in prescriptive 'do's' or 'don'ts'. The more deliberate the intention is the more direct the nexus between action and harm, the more avoidable also the injury, hence the greater the moral blame attaching to the harmful act. It is for this reason that we condemn even mere attempts to do harm, especially unsuccessful attempts to commit crimes. For these attempts portray an intention or desire to harm another person, an intention which, as the attempt shows, only failed because the agent was otherwise prevented, not because of a change in harmful intent. Similar are acts where A intends to harm B but injures C. In an old legal case, a clerk struck at his companion with the keys of the church; they flew out of his hand and out of the window, putting out a woman's eye; it was held mayhem 'because he had a bad intent at the beginning'.[13] Just as a mere attempt to do harm may be morally condemned, so an act like the above falls, though perhaps somewhat less easily, within the scope of moral fault. The clerk, admittedly, did not wish to hit the woman, let alone injure her grievously; but he was prepared to harm another; the harm to the woman was thus merely a consequence of an attempt at injury that was no less illegitimate. But for this circumstance, it would have been impossible to put any blame on the clerk for the injury caused by his keys.

Nor is this notion of avoidable harm confined to deliberately injurious acts. Harm can also be caused inadvertently, through a lack of appropriate care, otherwise known as carelessness or negligence. As this may range from recklessness to absent-mindedness, a moral theory would have to distinguish between the degree of negligence displayed: between a reckless ('I don't care') act on the one hand and a moment's distraction on the other to which even the most careful may be prone. Thus negligence offers an interesting instance of a sharply varying scale of moral blame as the degree of negligence will also be roughly indicative of the greater or lesser avoidability of the harm caused. By contrast there are actions which, even if intentional or deliberate, are yet not immediately or patently harmful, though capable of producing injurious consequences cumulatively or in the long run. Suppose A walks on B's lawn in disregard of a notice expressly prohibiting trespass at any time. Suppose that A's single trespass is utterly harmless, no visible damage being done (A may be wearing soft shoes, walking very carefully, without stamping the ground), also that the trespass occurs in the middle of the night, so remains entirely unnoticed and not an open encouragement for others to do the same. If we say that A's action is nevertheless wrong, the question is why. The only answer is that even if A is not doing actual harm he is still doing (what we may call) inchoate damage, in the sense that if everybody, or at least a sufficient number of others did the same, then damage would definitely ensue. This is one of many kinds of acts which, as Lyons has explained, do not produce identifiable damaging effects until certain thresholds are passed; we may not know exactly when this threshold effect will occur, but we do know, or can fairly infer, that each trespass is a contributory step towards it.[14]

Brief as this discussion has been, one can nevertheless see that a calculus of avoidable harm permits rational moral argument in two distinct, but closely related, respects. On the one hand, looking at agents and actions our argument is essentially about questions of responsibility, for it is to responsible agents that our moral rules address themselves. On the other hand, looking at the consequences of an action, at the harm done to another, our concern is with the nature of harm, with its effects or magnitude, or more broadly the extent to which one's wants or interests are detrimentally affected. Now questions relating to responsibility have to do with an agent's intentions, this being looked at from various points of view. First we are interested in his mental element or *mens rea* because this gives us perhaps the best clue of what the action was about, what, in particular, its avoidability was; for there is no point in blaming a person for causing harm if the harm is something he could not really avoid. We blame the agent not merely because the other person suffers but because the agent wishes or intends him to suffer, or because he was not careful enough to prevent such suffering. In this light we may even say, rather with Kant, that the good man is he who acts with a 'good' will. We do not have to think of the good man as 'good' in a sort of ultimate or essential sense, only in the more mundane sense of (broadly) 'good is as good does'; what, on this basis, therefore distinguishes a good from a bad will is simply the purpose with which an action is done. Accordingly, if the purpose is obviously to cause harm, it does not even have to succeed: which is the reason why mere attempts can be blameworthy and even punishable.[15]

As for questions relating to the harm itself, these go a somewhat different way. The principal question we now ask is not whether particular harm was avoidable with greater good will or care, but whether the harm is significant, in quality or quantity, so as to deserve blame or condemnation at all. What is, or is not, significant will of course depend on our shared attitudes; nor need the harm under consideration belong to a recognised category, for it can be of a new kind, provided it is harm giving rise to an intelligible grievance being something describable as a *malum in se*: that is, harm which we all know will cause pain, or at least a disadvantage, to another person as well as harm we are all likely to disapprove of or to resent, if only vicariously. Where the harm falls within an already recognised category its significance is not usually in dispute: we no longer argue whether harm resulting in loss of life or limb is serious harm, its gravity being completely taken for granted. However we do argue about what seem lesser injuries, or more controversial or debatable grievances, or new forms of harm, like new kinds of invasions of privacy or economic harm, which at an earlier stage were perhaps not regarded as instances of avoidable harm but rather as occasions of private misfortune or as acts of God. New and changing circumstances of life always bring with them new possibilities of harmful acts. Yet there are some liberties or immunities so basic to human beings that they are not affected by any passage of time. Your fist must always stop short of my face; could it go further moral argument would become utterly pointless, even if it were still possible.

HARM AS A BASIS OF MORALITY

Our calculus of avoidable harm may now be seen to coincide substantially with two more familiar moral ideas, that of justice and that of utility. It certainly coincides with classical utilitarianism for which there was little question that what made an action wrong was the infliction of pain or suffering. The classical utilitarians certainly gave much prominence also to pleasure; but in the area of conduct we are now discussing it is the negative version devoted to the minimisation of pain that is the dominant principle. For Bentham, in particular, forbearance from harm or mischief to others

constitutes a sort of primary 'duty of probity', just as the
principle of avoiding pain furnishes (for him) a general
standard of utility for judging actions, instead of 'a mere
principle in words, a kind of phrase' that expresses nothing
more than an 'unfounded sentiment' or 'caprice'. For
Bentham, consequently, only such a utilitarian principle
would allow us to reason cogently, for only this provides 'the
standard of right and wrong', not just purely personal reasons
that are anyhow either 'despotical' or 'anarchical'.[16]

The coincidence with justice seems a little more difficult.
For it is nowadays thought that doing harm to others has
little or nothing to do with justice. Murder, it is said (for
example), though morally wrong, is not exactly unjust, at
least in the current sense of justice in which it is primarily a
distributive idea; what, accordingly, is wrong with murder is
'that a man is *killed*, not that *he*, rather than somebody else,
is'.[17] Now it is certainly true that it is in the distributive area
that justice does its more distinctive work. Even so, justice is
not exclusively distributive if only because one of its basic
ingredients is the notion of equality which can be infringed
not only by some maldistribution but also by an act of injury.
So in murder the relevant equality infringed is not between
the person killed and another, but between the killer and the
killed. What makes the killing unjust is that one person is
made the victim of another; the victim is, so to speak, used
unequally, the killer elevating himself above the other person
in complete disregard of the latter's liberty or immunity: the
killer, as Kant would say, uses the victim as a means to an
end—his own end—and so gives to the victim a lesser value
than to himself. If the whole point of just conduct is, as surely
it is, to act with full respect for the equal value of each
individual, this must mean at the very least that one cannot be
deprived of life or limb by the unilateral interventions of
another. Even the word 'injustice' is closely connected with
'injury'; in fact, 'injury' did not originally mean only, as it
does now, actual harm done or suffered; more interestingly it
meant harm done *in jura*, that is, 'against rights', or more

broadly, harm done by one person's 'superior' disregard of another's integrity or immunity, thus by one person's assumption of superiority over another, what the Greeks called *hybris*.

It may be objected that in so closely associating morality, or at any rate one form of morality, with avoidable harm, we are not facing what may be thought to be the one real question, namely, why we should or ought to be moral at all. However, as earlier hinted, this question is not really answerable as it stands, any more than one can answer why one should be prudential or wise if one prefers not to be. The more helpful question is the purely rational one, namely, as to the lines along which moral reasoning can proceed, or the tenable reasons one can give in a moral argument. It is to answer this that we have been so concerned to elucidate the logical features of the moral judgements we make, including the moral grounds on which we can assess a grievance or judge an action to be right or wrong. As we have also seen, our moral reasons do not relate to means but to ends; and while personal ends must differ so long as we wish to act as free or self-realising men, these ends are obviously bound to collide unless they are limited or restricted at the point at which collisions would otherwise occur: which, logically, is precisely the point at which we begin to speak of mutual harm. In this way an approach through avoidable harm directly responds to what must be the basic aim of any moral theory, namely, to protect a person's basic liberty or immunity, thereby also protecting his most basic interests.

This concern with harm is fully evident in the life we lead and the language we speak. To imagine a society without a notion of harm or injury, we would have to think of a form of social life without disputes or even grievances, without a concept of 'right' or 'want' or 'responsible action' as well as without such notions as 'obligation' or 'ought'. Human beings, Hobbes remarked, are not the only creatures living 'sociably'; bees and ants, too, live together 'naturally' so long as not offended by their fellows; yet whereas they only react to immediate pain, men also distinguish 'injury'.[18] That is to say, they distinguish between, on the one hand, damage left to purely 'private' anger or revenge and, on the other hand, damage that does constitute an offence in terms of the injurious norms of a group, thus also calls for 'public' or 'social' responses wherever the group recognises the injury as an occasion for blame and for counter-measures befitting the damage or injury done. Nor could we imagine such social responses unless we could concomitantly presuppose interests or 'values' which we happen to share as a human group. So unless we can presuppose an overall social norm directed against the infliction of avoidable harm, vague and abstract though that norm is; unless (to put it another way) we can presuppose a social preference for injury-free conduct or an injury-immune life within a group, and can presuppose this not just as a logical condition but also as a condition that faithfully reflects an actual social fact, moral discourse about actions would not be, nor would ever have been, practicable.

4 Distributive Justice and Utility

PROBLEMS OF DISTRIBUTION

We proceed to look at another group of moral grievances all broadly concerned with the distribution of burdens and benefits. Unless we do separate questions of distribution from those of avoidable harm we shall fail to see that distributive discourse raises many new considerations with quite a different structure of argument. Where the preceding chapter dealt with avoidable and responsible actions, the present also includes complex states of affairs for which no individual agent is directly blamable. Where we earlier dealt with what is done to us, our business now is with what (we think) is due to us, the burdens we reject, the advantages we wish to keep or acquire. Where questions about avoidable harm came together in a single and uniform model, distributive questions extend over a very varied continuum which at one end raises questions which are quite firmly answerable but at the other end poses questions to which the relevant answers remain incorrigibly 'open' and changeable. Again, where our calculus of avoidable harm comfortably absorbed notions of justice and utility, in the sense that the latter did not raise separate issues (the whole thrust of the argument there obviously being that the infliction of harm cannot be either morally just or utilitarian), problems of distribution give to both justice and utility a far more conspicuous role, if only because these notions now serve, respectively, as focal points that assemble many of the questions we do and must ask in any rational discussion of distributive grievances.

But why are distributive questions so different? The answer is relatively simple. Complaints which derive from physical harm, injuries to an eye or an arm (for example), are more easily assessed than grievances about some maldistribution of the goods of life where it is by no means clear whether or why, or to what extent, a person should have the same social or economic advantages as another person, or why, correspondingly, he should have less or should have more. An eye or arm forms part of a person, of his 'organic' whole, much as his eye or arm may differ from another's in health or strength or skill; to inflict bodily harm is then not only to interfere with that person, it is visibly to diminish him; man such as he is now becomes, as it were, the measure both of himself and of all other men. In the case of distribution, on the other hand, we have no such 'organic' measure or unit. Once we go beyond the most basic needs, those a person must satisfy in order simply to survive, other material benefits or advantages can be distributed in a variety of ways. Unlike our sensations of harm and pain which do not change (if they did the human race would perhaps also change as a race), we can all have different ideas from time to time about which or how many of the goods of life we wish to have each of us or as a community. Not that our options are here unlimited, for where the goods of life are scarce as we have to assume they are (because if richly abundant no distributive problem would arise), there are in fact not so many things we can do. We can distribute or share out what there is either equally or unequally, and we may do one or the other either because as a group we have agreed to do so, or failing this in order to satisfy human needs, or to reward desert or merit, or to promote the public interest. These, singly or in combination, are in fact our only options, there are no other distributive possibilities.

Still, to identify these options is yet to say nothing about their respective weights or priorities. Indeed, looked at severally, these options can easily get into conflict. So a distribution according to desert may conflict with one according to need, while as private interests both may be opposed to a public interest. Still more importantly, our basic distributive intuitions appear somehow at odds: on the one hand, it seems decidedly counterintuitive to suggest that people can, morally, be treated unequally; on the other, we seem to agree, no less intuitively, that to treat people justly or rightly is not always to treat them the same; our very recognition of need and desert confirms just this possible inequality. Even so, we shall come to see that these options are not quite so irreconcilable as at first they appear, provided we see them not as self-evident or self-sufficient revelations about certain situations, not as revelations only vouchsafed to those intuitively endowed, but see them rather as the rational grounds or reasons with which we need to support our distributive choices or decisions; moreover grounds which can be so coordinated as to form part of a coherent moral theory. In this way we no longer have to rely on intuitions alone which are in any case incomplete premises for moral reasoning; incomplete not so much because they only express our feelings or attitudes, for moral discourse could not even begin without critical attitudes that initiate as well as 'energise' our grievances; incomplete, rather, because intuitions only report our preferences without providing anything like a theoretical framework that can serve as a check on our intuitions, apt as these are to diverge and to fluctuate.

To see further why intuitions alone do not suffice, consider the simple case of two parties buying a bar of chocolate to the price of which they contribute equally. Suppose we intuitively conclude that half a bar for each is the only distribution we could possibly consider as the 'just' or 'right' one. But why should this be so? How would we explain to a morally ignorant person (assuming such a person is nevertheless capable of understanding our present problem) why each party cannot morally claim more than a half-share? So we might say, falling back on our intuitive common sense, that

(1) half a bar is the only 'just' distribution, or (2) half is here the only possible 'fair' share, or (3) each getting half is the 'best' solution as it maximises the satisfaction of each side. However to say one or even all these things does not really add anything very helpful. For one thing, the three intuitive responses amount to virtually the same thing: clearly there is now little or no difference between (1) and (2); even (3) is dependent on (1) or (2) in that if we cannot understand (1) or (2) we cannot understand (3), for it would be nonsensical to say that each regards an equal division as (for him) the best or most satisfactory if at the same time each regards that distribution as (for him) unjust or unfair. For another and more important thing, what in this particular example makes anything other than a half-share 'unjust' or 'wrong' is that each party obviously agreed to buy, and accordingly contributed to, half a share; their cooperative intent was for them to share equally. It is this agreement which provides the standard by which the injustice or unfairness is now judged, just as it is this 'contractarian' standard which defines the possible disadvantage in respect of which, in circumstances such as these, a complaint can be made. For while one cannot complain about the other getting less than oneself, one can and does complain about the other getting more: 'more' now meaning the specifiable disadvantage arising from one benefiting at the other's expense. If, for example, the two sides had contributed in different proportions (one contributing two-thirds of the price, the other only one-third), it is clear that a distribution by halves would have been unjust to the two-thirds contributor. So that, here again, our distributive judgement, far from being simply intuitive, greatly depends on the 'contractarian' standard supplied by the parties' own intentions or what we take to be their intentions.

We shall later identify other 'contractarian' standards when we turn to deal with distributive problems that arise in selective groups or in connection with cooperative practices. For the present we are more concerned with situations where we do not have anything like a contractarian or cooperative base, where (in other words) we have no indication whatever either from the parties themselves or from the recognised ideals of their group or society how the available goods of life are to be shared out. Here, too, as already said, we can opt for either an equal or an unequal distribution. But how do we decide which it is to be? Excluding public interest (as, for the moment, we are still only discussing purely private or individual claims), the only distributive options still left open are those of desert or need. With these options we must deal first, particularly since, opposed to each other as they obviously are, they yet constitute logically adjacent notions (one begins where the other stops), thus also notions that logically complement each other as they enable us to see on both sides of the line when confronted with perhaps our most significant distributive alternatives.

NEEDS AND EQUALITY

We shall argue that, speaking broadly, a claim based on need is essentially a claim for equality and that, furthermore, one cannot tenably advance a claim of need, i.e. advance arguable reasons for it, except in very special circumstances, broadly of two sorts: where the claim is made as a matter of sheer survival or as a matter of adjusting certain natural or fortuitous differences between people. Why need offers only so restricted a claim is perhaps best argued with the help of an example. Take a group of a hundred persons, all starving, yet in the possession of a hundred loaves of bread, a quantity we suppose to be sufficient to still the immediate hunger of all. We assume that theirs is a sudden misfortune, that the hundred never envisaged such a situation nor agreed what should be done were it to arise. The only thing they do agree on is that they wish to do what is morally just or right, if only because they regard themselves as all belonging to one universe of moral discourse in which claims or grievances are not dismissed with a shrug, but are seriously argued or reasoned about. How, then, can they argue and, after argument, reasonably conclude as to what should now be the right distribution?

A first step would be to say that, as in any other moral dispute, the participants in the above example must argue universalisably: that when one of the hundred asks for his needs to be met, these needs cannot be just his needs alone, but have to be the needs of persons of a class or kind. If he admits that that class comprises all the hundred persons, he *eo ipso* admits that they must all be treated equally, so that each will get one loaf of bread. But universalisability, as a purely formal requirement, does not commit us to such a solution of total equality; for we may argue, no less universalisably, on behalf of a smaller class: we may say, for instance, that fifty persons constitute a 'superior' class therefore requiring two loaves each, no matter what happens to the others. It follows that universalisability not only fails to give us a complete argument regarding the distributive choice we would now accept, but that to complete the argument we have to identify further facts in the situation. But what facts? Another example may help us here. Suppose that one A, neither starving nor poor, demands of another (B), one of two loaves of bread B just bought for himself. If they happen to be friends, more or less, B might be regarded as impolite were he to refuse the request, yet his refusal could not, most would agree, be criticised as 'unjust' or 'unfair' or even as 'disutilitarian', even if this refusal may cause the friendship to terminate. However, if now we ask why in the first example we support a distribution based on needs, while in the second example we do not, the distinction should be obvious. In the first the loaf of bread is a matter of survival, in the second at most a matter of convenience for the other man. What, in the first example, convinces us that distribution should be equal, or substantially equal, is that to enable each person here to survive each requires one loaf on average; only an equal distribution thus appears to us 'just' or 'right' since only an equal sharing will look after the bare necessities of each starving member of the group. The second example exhibits no such needs of survival; if the other man wants or needs bread he can buy it as did his friend. Had needs been really involved, had (for example) one friend been in dire need of bread while the other had one loaf too many, an equal sharing of the two loaves would have been, here too, the only just and right distribution.

Somewhat similar considerations can be seen to apply to the familiar case of the drowning man. Suppose A sees B drowning in shallow water: is A under moral duty to answer B's call for help? We assume that though A runs no risk to himself in helping B, except for some slight inconvenience, mainly getting wet, he yet refuses to do anything. Yet ready as we are to criticise A, on what grounds can we do so? One will observe that A has done nothing to cause B's dire predicament; nor has A ever promised to help, nor (we also suppose) is there an established rule or practice in this particular community requiring A to help. It follows that the only remaining ground on which a claim of help can be based is B's extreme need, the threat to his very survival. A's helping hand now is, in point of time, even more urgent than was the loaf of bread in the earlier example. In fact for A to refuse to help, at so little cost to himself, can even be seen as something like doing deliberate harm to B; A's refusal to help is difficult to explain except by supposing that A harbours a harmful intention towards B, or so callous an indifference to B's survival as to make A's intentions no less harmful. Just as an attempt to kill (as we saw in chapter 3) is a morally reprehensible and punishable act, so an omission to avert a death is morally condemnable, perhaps even more so because of the fatal consequences now ensuing. Of course if a man does not understand the special need of a starving or drowning man, it may be no good to argue with him. If a man does understand, he may still reject his moral duty, just as he can reject any other moral (or legal) duty, but he will then have to face the heteronomous censure of the community.

What the drowning-man case also brings out is that certain distributive situations closely resemble those of avoidable harm we discussed earlier. A failure to help is of course not exactly like doing harm, it is rather an omission to distribute one's own time and labour on behalf of another. Nevertheless where, as here, a failure to help has, manifestly and immediately, deadly consequences, though also easily avoidable ones, a distinction between doing and not helping becomes morally pointless. Bentham was therefore right to regard a callous failure to help as an extension of doing harm.[1] Our previous hundred starving men can be seen in the same light. What made their needs so special and urgent was the danger that they would all perish without bread. To refuse bread to any of them was thus as sure, even if perhaps not quite so quick, a way of causing death as was A's refusal to help B. We therefore see that needs become ever more 'special' or urgent the greater or more immediate the possibility of physical harm.

To put the emphasis, as we now do, on special or extreme need also helps to put the canon of equality in a proper perspective. The equal distribution under which, as in our earlier example, everyone gets one loaf of bread represents not an absolute but a *prima facie* rule; it meets the fact that equal distribution will *on average* look after the immediate needs of each starving member of the group. Our egalitarian presumption, accordingly, by no means excludes certain departures from it, if only because some people do in fact have greater needs than others: adults need more food than small children, sick people a little more than healthy ones, and so forth. Indeed by taking into account a person's actual needs we even convert a purely formal or bare equality into a more 'substantive' or 'real' one, for equality does not always mean, or have to mean, that everyone gets the same amount, but only that everyone will be kept alive or kept going at the same rate. A man in danger may need and receive more protection than an unthreatened man; what is important is not that he is receiving more attention than the other, but that he is made equally secure.[2] So Aristotle insisted on proportionate rather than simple equality; he saw a distribution as just not where everyone is treated equally, but where the distributive ratio or proportion is the same for everyone.[3] The emphasis on extreme needs also implies that a person can advance only claims for such needs which he cannot by his own efforts take care of, as where he is too sick or too young or too incapacitated to look after himself. This further means that such needs must arise in conditions of extreme rather than usual scarcity, the latter being, of course, the conditions in which most of us find ourselves most of the time. Here it is for the claimant himself to satisfy his needs as it is for everyone to earn his living as best he can or will. For in conditions of usual scarcity the immediate issue is not survival, but rather how we improve, or at any rate maintain, our standard of living, which is a matter of desert rather than need. Indeed to distinguish between these conditions is to indicate the essential milieu in which desert and need can each play its own distinctive role.

What we have said about needs may lend a new perspective to the relationship between justice and utility, as it allows us to see them as far less opposed to each other than is often believed; it should no longer surprise us that our views of what is just do not here have to be at all in conflict with our utilitarian beliefs. For if we take utilitarianism as a moral (as distinct from a purely prudential or expedient) principle, it too must start, for all its concern with a community's total or general happiness, from the ground-rule upon which (Mill tells us) Bentham already insisted, namely, that everyone is to count as one and no more than one.[4] This ground-rule introduces the same egalitarian element on which justice builds, being also very similar to what Kant meant in his second formulation of the categorical imperative, that none is to use another person solely as his means. To see this better consider again our earlier example of the hundred starving men: suppose sixty of them vote or allocate to themselves all the hundred loaves, leaving nothing for the other forty. In doing this the sixty would scarcely act or decide morally, according to a rule applying to everyone; they would instead be adopting what Bentham called a 'despotical' decision as they impose their own satisfaction while disregarding that of the rest. It is possible that the sixty may be doing the wrong thing also from a strictly economic point of view, in that in taking the hundred loaves the sixty may take more for their own satisfaction than they actually need, a distribution therefore caught by the law of diminishing utility compared with the greater utility that could be achieved by giving all the hundred one loaf each.[5] Whether this is so or not on economic grounds, the point remains that the utilitarian argument, if looked at as a moral and not a prudential argument, cannot permit the sixty to treat themselves as counting, each one of them, as more than one; even the maxim of the greatest happiness of the greatest number cannot morally allow that only sixty will live while forty go under, so long as it is possible that all hundred can survive. To disregard the welfare of anyone for the greater benefit only of the majority would be to sacrifice the basic egalitarian principle certainly not on moral, at best only on expedient, grounds. If this is so, justice and utility cannot but lead to the same result in that both require an equal distribution wherever urgent human needs require this, just as both can depart from strict equality where the beneficiaries differ in their actual needs, so as to give (for example) the very young a little less bread and adults a little more.

Once this is seen it also cannot be true what is often asserted, namely, that utility striving to attain the best for the greatest number can countenance what justice with its individualistic bias cannot, namely, endorse certain departures from basic human equality, departures such as, to give the two most familiar examples, the institution of slavery or the exemplary punishment of the innocent. For if what we said about the utilitarians' ground-rule is sound, these departures would simply not be permissible, because by enslaving a minority, the majority would 'despotically' impose their own satisfaction to the detriment of that of the minority; the majority would thus not act according to a moral rule for this must apply to the whole group which includes everyone. Utilitarians sometimes suggest that, under their doctrine, it could still be better to increase a group's total happiness even if this means giving less happiness to the minority. But, surely, this is what our ground-rule disallows; the majority cannot leave the minority, now enslaved, with what amounts to quite insufficient happiness. A whole group, it is true, may politically decide to give each member less for the sake of a greater common good; this is a very different policy, as we shall later see; what is now denied is that a majority can make slaves of the minority, even on utilitarian grounds; and a somewhat similar argument protects the innocent. Under certain circumstances it may well be the case that an exemplary punishment could very effectively deter offenders of all kinds. Of such salutary effects we might even greatly approve, but it would be approval on mainly empirical grounds, as a result of such a policy actually proving a successful one. Not only moral acts, but prudential results, too, are capable of being approved or commended, just as we often approve of or applaud things of beauty or elegance, or artistic or athletic accomplishments; which, incidentally, again shows that policies or purposes cannot qualify as moral merely on account of their being commended or approved. Thus the punishment of the innocent, highly successful and applauded as it might otherwise be, turns out to be utterly at odds with a strictly moral point of view, precisely because it destroys a fundamental distinction on which moral arguments must rest, namely that between (broadly) guilt and innocence; it is a distinction without which any inquiry into moral responsibility becomes as ridiculous as it would be futile.

DESERT, MERIT AND INEQUALITY

Moral considerations about desert or merit are, in many ways, far more pervasive than claims concerning one's special needs or vital necessities. In fact questions of desert mainly arise in conditions we earlier described as those of 'usual' scarcity, including the socioeconomic inequalities to which such conditions give rise. These are inequalities, moreover, which do not normally result from any individual action but from historically complex and often fortuitous events that in turn create social states of affairs which cannot be altered except, if at all, by collective or socially organised measures, by the group or society acting as a body politic. Especially is this so in large societies, the city or state, where people simply happen, rather than plan, to live together, and where they may so live without sharing a common purpose, let alone a set of cooperative or 'fraternal' values—quite unlike the members of a small or selective group in which each member's benefit or burden is more or less clearly defined by the group's agreed objective or common ideology or their specific enterprise. Even a larger group, needless to say, may adopt common values if not for all then for some of its activities, and if they do they will have more or less definite standards for deciding what any one individual's share should be. Where this occurs the state of course changes from a non-selective to a selective group.

However the principal problem now confronting us is how we are to cope with distributive grievances in a non-selective society, one in which the prevailing conditions of usual scarcity give it a predominantly acquisitive or competitive character. The precise question here always comes back to this: can a poor man advance grounds for saying that he should be less poor than he is; or, putting this more broadly, can a beggar claim a contribution as of moral right instead of appealing to our pity or charity? The answer to this comes in two parts. A very poor man can certainly make a claim to the bare necessities of life, to allow him not to get richer but to survive if starving, or to be medically looked after if dangerously or seriously ill. Even a non-selective society lacking common moral values still recognises that at any rate as between members of the same group some moral duties or rights obtain. It was on this ground that our group of a hundred starving men had to share their hundred loaves; that ten or sixty or even ninety members in this group could not take all the hundred loaves, leaving nothing for the rest. The second part of our answer follows directly from the implicit limitations of the first. Suppose our poor man is claiming not bare necessities but a greater share of the goods of life; it would be a juster society, he might well say, if the goods of life were shared more equally, his own needs being no less great than those of persons more fortunate than he. Unfortunately this is a claim he cannot now convincingly sustain, nor is it difficult to understand why this seemingly heartless answer has to be what it is. The simple explanation is that we are still within a context of usual scarcity with the result that whatever there is not only comes from the efforts of others, efforts that significantly differ from man to man, but from efforts which still produce only a limited stock. Hence what there is is still not enough to give everyone a relatively large slice: there may be sufficient to supply a modicum perhaps for many but not for all. And since the poor man is now asking not just a minor but a substantial improvement of his standard of life, if only because a minor improvement would still leave him poor, his full claim becomes impossible of fulfilment, the cake being too small. It also turns out that if his claim were given effect to, it would penalise those other members of the group who worked harder or better to provide what there is.

Given these conditions, our only distributive option, for no other would strike us as just or right, is to reward each person according to his contribution, which is why we say that a person is rewarded according to what he merits or deserves, according to what is in this sense due to him. On this principle a person gets more because he contributes more, quantitatively or qualitatively, just as one contributing less will get less—not that this principle can confidently tell us how much exactly he does deserve, the difficulty being to quantify the cash value of what he deserves or what in each case his 'wage-justice' should be. We may think, for instance, that in matters of health the surgeon makes a larger contribution than the nurse, and both perhaps a larger contribution than the kitchen-staff, 'larger' having regard to the work done, the skill and knowledge required and so on. Even here the difficulty however is that the value of these contributions cannot, often enough, be assessed without taking into account other factors as well. The work of a surgeon cannot be assessed simply in relation to his professional virtues (his industry, devotion to duty etc.), we also need to know something of his socioeconomic 'utility', the supply and demand of doctors as well as the social importance we attach to medical progress or to public health. So what a surgeon can be said to deserve will depend both on ideas of justice and of utility since we have to consider both his personal accomplishments and his 'social' value or usefulness, that is, his value in the market-place or in an economic plan. Hence in relation to merit or desert, ideas of justice and utility, far from competing become in fact complementary, weaving in and out of each other as we try to translate into money the exact value of what people do and deserve.

It may be objected that in so presenting the role of desert an important moral problem is all too easily over-looked. If we say that the achiever justly or rightly deserves more than the non-contributor, what becomes of the man who expends a great deal of effort yet whose rewards are ridiculously small by comparison. A classical composer may produce works which though highly labour-intensive command a low price as there is no great demand for them. And if so, does this not mean that utilitarian considerations may bring about results we may think to be unjust? If so, again, does this not also mean that justice is morally superior to utility, if only because justice pays particular heed to individual effort while utility seems to look more at supply and demand? This objection is less strong than appears at first sight. Admittedly justice is concerned to reward effort according to personal merit, but it is a reward that has to come out of the goods of life that others produce. The claim for a just (or 'juster') reward so becomes a claim that others reward you justly which, however, is a claim you cannot press unless the others also get something which *they* want; for since the just reward that is to come to you consists, at least in part, of something they produce, their claim from you is no less valid than your claim from them. Hence even if we confined ourselves to an approach through justice, we would still have to come to terms with this conflicting consideration: that while you 'deserve' things from others, the others may also have deserving claims against you. And once we take, as we must, 'desert' in this commutative sense, utilitarian considerations of the kind here considered are no longer far behind.

There remains another point. Merely to say that one merits or deserves more than another only because one works harder, or because one is a better producer or achiever, is not as yet a sufficient argument. For to claim that one deserves more than the next fellow is not only to say that one works harder or better than the other, it is also to say that the other refuses to give a similar account of himself. Conversely, you cannot argue that you deserve more than the other when the other lacks the opportunity to compete with you in effort and achievement on equal terms. If a career is not open to all the talents, you cannot say that you *deserve* its prizes when others of equal merit are prevented from entering it. Equality of opportunity thus reveals itself as an essential condition without which, it is now obvious, one cannot even begin to advance claims of merit or desert. Without equal opportunity a rich reward would not qualify as deserving; it would rather be like winning a game in which the other competitor is denied any chance to win.

But, it will then be asked, what about the person who is too sick or too physically or mentally handicapped? For him, equality of opportunity is plainly irrelevant, since he, being incapacitated, cannot seize the opportunity however promising. Against such a person, it is true, it would be wholly inappropriate to claim anything on the basis of desert or opportunity since the achiever cannot compare his effort, let alone his desert, with that of anyone incapable of competing. Still the point is that the sick or handicapped would have no claim against the producer anyhow being himself a non-producer. As a non-producer, furthermore, the only claim he can advance is one based on need, that is, his need to survive or subsist though unable to earn even the barest minimum necessary. Persons in real and urgent need, we earlier maintained, do have a claim to some help or assistance, since we do take it to be just and right to do what is necessary not to let them go under. Indeed the actual amount of such help can vary at different times; it seems that we have more generous ideas as to what constitutes 'minimal welfare' or 'subsistence' in periods of affluence than in times of economic depression; the concept of 'need' or 'necessities of life' thus can fluctuate from bread and water to three square meals a day to sometimes even a little more. Within these parameters, however, this is all that a claim of need can be, while outside these parameters a claim for a share of the goods of life can only be a claim for reward according to what one's contributions merit or deserve.[6]

DISTRIBUTIVE SCHEMES: UNFAIR ADVANTAGES

We return to distributive grievances that arise in what we have called 'contractarian' contexts. Such are the disputes arising in selective, usually smaller, groups, or groups the members of which engage in some cooperative enterprise. Where two or more persons agree to pursue a joint or common venture to achieve an objective not achieveable otherwise than by multiple and cooperative effort, they will, of necessity, share a broadly common scheme based on what the cooperative venture is about. Suppose several persons combine or pool their skills to bring about, by team-work, a specific task (T), and suppose that one of these (let us call him D, the recalcitrant member) fails to act cooperatively at a crucial moment of time, thus at once giving rise to the question of what arguments may be advanced to blame D, or what argument D may use in order to excuse his failure to act.

Suppose, for example, that D, a member of a four-man relay team refuses to run or swim his allotted length. We would now say that D has let the side down, that he has severely disappointed the expectations of the other three. A person like D puts himself, here deliberately so, in the position of someone breaking a promise since he breaks the team's common agreement to do T; D clearly undertook to do his stretch, but then failed to do so at the last moment when, as we further assume, alternative arrangements were no longer possible. Let us also suppose that D cannot advance an acceptable excuse, such as a sudden illness or injury, but that D's failure causes no actual harm to the other three, meaning discernible physical or financial harm, this being a sort of voluntary enterprise, not one intended to earn money in which latter case a failure to cooperate would certainly involve financial loss. Even so, D's act causes disappointment enough to amount to something significantly hurtful to the other members of the team, be it only the hurt to their expectations or sensitivities, not to mention the possibly great inconvenience done to them. On such facts, we have again a situation somewhat similar to one of avoidable harm in that D's failure to co-operate brings about the collapse of an agreed or shared enterprise. It is indeed just this deliberately disutilitarian act (using the word 'utilitarian' now in an instrumental sense) that explains the grievance of the other three; why they say that D's act was unfair or unjust or wrong. The other three can now blame D for a certain harm as their comparative positions have been detrimentally affected in that the three expended personal resources (time and effort) to achieve a common benefit now inexcusably frustrated by the action of the fourth.

Consider next a situation where a failure to cooperate may again be judged as eminently unfair even though the total enterprise does not collapse. Imagine four men in a boat who have spent the day on a river excursion and are now on their way home; while three of them row back energetically, the fourth (F) refuses to lend a hand, this on the ground that the other three can manage as effectively as the four of them would; nothing, F says, would be gained even if he rowed nor any harm done if he rested. If what F says is factually correct, how can we say that he behaves unfairly? Even if the other three are far from indifferent to F's inactivity, on what grounds can they object? In fact their only ground is that F is taking an unscheduled advantage over them. If F may feel like having a rest, this may be no less true of the others; why, then, should he have the benefit (of the excursion) without making the contribution expected from him.[7] Nor does it now matter that the advantage taken by F is (as we assume) inconsequential as his contributory rowing is anyhow not necessary for the task in hand. It does not matter because the moral argument against F is based on the parties' relative advantages. Though the common task does not collapse, F's refusal to cooperate means not only that F is getting a benefit without a corresponding burden, thus getting something for nothing; F is also introducing a new element by unilaterally, almost self-elevatingly, putting himself above his fellows with whom he had agreed, if not explicitly at any rate implicitly, to share all common tasks, only barring some unforeseen contingency such as illness or incapacity.

Still, without an element of actual harm or injury, the argument of unfairness seems at first sight very weak. For since F can say that what he did made no practical difference, the charge of unfairness looks more of an empty charge, or if not exactly empty, a trifling and minor complaint about which one does not go to war or go to court: a court of law may regard this as eminently a case of *de minimis non curat lex*. Yet though admittedly minor, the complaint of unfairness nevertheless stands, except that the complaint being minor the social consequences of our moral disapproval will now be relatively minor too. Thus we may condemn F's behaviour as revealing a flaw in his character and leave it at that; or we may decide not to ask him again to join in a collaborative enterprise as he is not the sort of companion we may seek out for joint ventures even of only a recreational kind. For some, such an unflattering testimonial is moral condemnation enough; that is why they will try to limit or to reinterpret the alleged agreement to cooperate, or they may seek to exculpate themselves by admitting the charge of unfairness but by advancing some excuse, that is, by pointing to supervening considerations that may at least extenuate their full responsibility. For others, however, moral disapproval will have little effect and for them we require the punitive or coercive measures of the law. Still, legal intervention merely reinforces yet does not replace the moral argument, for we still need to know what the moral argument is as well as whether the moral blame is greater or smaller before we can know whether, or to what extent, the law should intervene at all.

What we have said about the relay team or the four men in the boat is not confined to leisurely activities. There are many other examples of people enjoying advantages which we have grounds to call unfair, even in situations which do not begin with an agreement to cooperate. There are many social practices, many groups large and small, with quite definite cooperative requirements. Trade unions would never succeed unless workmen readily combined for their joint purposes. Hence the so-called 'free-rider', the person refusing to pay his union dues while accepting increased wages obtained through the effort of more loyal unionists, can be said to get a benefit he does nothing to procure. Not all workers need to strike to produce better conditions even in

one branch of industry, just as not all four were needed to
bring back the boat. The fact remains that unionists strike to
improve their own conditions, not the conditions of those
who forsake their cause; hence the resentment against the
free-rider lies in his getting a benefit for which others, but not
he, needed to make a special sacrifice. A comparable
resentment works against someone attempting to jump a
queue. Since we cannot all enter a bus or buy a ticket at once,
we have to line up, form a queue, so as to stagger or rotate the
scarce things or services we here seek. The most spontaneous
or voluntary way of lining up is obviously to adhere to a
system of first come, first served. Where the merits or the
'equities' are equal, says an old legal maxim, the first in time
prevails. In the queue the person ahead of you has the
prevailing equity that he has waited longer than the person
behind. And with our advantages thus lined up or ordered,
those upsetting it behave unfairly precisely because they try
to take an unfair advantage over those who have waited
longer, so have expended greater effort to obtain the things
only available successively. Here, moreover, the familiar saw
'if everybody did the same' becomes particularly relevant. It
makes us see what we often forget, that lining-up is an
essential procedure if an advantage is to be got in an orderly
way where many people simultaneously compete for it.

These observations may begin to throw a little further
light on the notion of fairness itself: why, more particularly,
certain acts are described as 'unfair' rather than as 'unjust'. An
unfairness, we now see, consists of a failure to cooperate in a
process or activity by which scarce or hard-to-get advantages
are realisable or obtainable. [8] Unionists need to cooperate to
produce the strength of numbers. Queues are necessary to
distribute successive advantages. Similarly the 'unfair' spo-
rtsman is one who fails to cooperate in playing the game in
that he refuses his rival a chance of winning, though this is
mainly because of a lack of generosity for which the rules do
not actually provide. On the other hand, a charge of
unfairness is out of place if some people merely happen to

find themselves in a more advantageous position than others. A handicapped person cannot accuse of unfairness those naturally more endowed. Nor, to take a more difficult example, can a soldier maimed in war accuse of unfairness those too old or too young who stayed at home, even though they enjoy the fruits of victory which the soldiers made possible. There is, Broad said, 'no relevant difference between you and those who join which entitles you to the halfpence without the kicks and them to the certainty of the kicks and the possibility of no halfpence'.[9] Though this is true, even tragically true, the fact remains that those taking the halfpence without the kicks are not responsible for the windfall coming to them; there is nothing they could have done either to refuse this particular halfpence or to avoid the kicks to the soldiers. To accuse people of behaving unfairly implies the possibility that people *could* have behaved fairly had they chosen so to act.

PRIVATE AND PUBLIC INTERESTS

So far, we will have noticed, the ideas or intuitions associated with 'justice' or 'utility' did not lead to different distributive results. The fact remains that there is a residual difference between them, justice being principally concerned with the claims of the individual as an individual, while utility can and often does draw attention to the demands of the group or society collectively. This difference however does not so much reflect an intrinsic conflict between these notions themselves as, rather, a divergence between two ultimate interests of distribution, that is, between our individual and our collective interests. Indeed this tension between in- dividual and collective interests can be seen in the notion of 'justice' or that of 'utility' itself, since both notions can be taken in a narrower and a wider sense; the narrower sense somehow always on a collision course with the wider; the former more individual-oriented, the latter rather stressing the general good. So justice (usually in the guise of 'social justice') may put its emphasis not on individual but more on social demands or 'average' satisfactions,[10] while utility, too, may become more attentive to individual than public interests. Yet however this may be, it is still the case that, traditionally at any rate, utility or utilitarianism is more closely connected with ideas of the common good or public interest. This is perhaps mainly because of its felicific feature, often considered to give utilitarianism its distinctive edge, and according to which actions or affairs are judged by their aggregative consequences, how they increase or maximise the amount of total (social) happiness.

In this light, justice and utility can be viewed as supporting opposing interests, especially where there arises a clear conflict between private and public demands, between (for example) some wanting something (say, bread today) and others wanting something else (bread and jam tomorrow). The conflict here is between equally legitimate interests: the individual's interest to get his just reward on the one hand, society's interest in accumulating industrial capital and production on the other. The individual, it need hardly be said, has a deep interest in immediately getting his full reward, life being what it is as well as short, whereas society, taking a longer view, may wish to attack the very conditions of scarcity. Nor are these conflicts easily resolved. Without draconian measures, all we can do is to seek some political agreement or consensus or compromise as to how our social wealth is to be produced and shared. In fact much of our political process is designed to facilitate such agreements as it pushes towards bringing otherwise endless disagreements to an at any rate temporary halt through (typically majoritarian) decision-procedures that settle our distributive policies at least for a time.

There is another sense in which a public interest may differ from a private one. A public interest may intervene not, as before, to override the interests of the private citizen in favour of the common good, but now to resolve a deadlock between two private interests of equal weight. To resolve such a deadlock we may have to look at the wider social repercussions of a decision by trying to gauge its possible effect on other parties besides those immediately involved. It is in assessing such wider consequences that we identify a 'public interest', the latter now rather representing a sort of estimate of whether, or how seriously, these consequences affect a larger or smaller segment of other people as well. And such an inquiry will obviously be pre-eminently utilitarian in character; indeed we shall shortly see that in this area of public interest only a notion of utility, no longer one of justice, can be of help at all.

As a simple illustration consider a dispute between two neighbours, A and B. Suppose A wants to play the piano while B wants to take his rest next door. A has a right to do what he wants on his premises, just as B has a right to do his thing in his own place. Can B insist that A stop his musical activities? Complaints of this kind, frequent enough in the law, raise the technical question whether A's conduct constitutes what is called a 'nuisance', that is, an 'unreasonable' interference with B's use and enjoyment of his land. Of course in trying to decide such a question we have to have some idea of what a 'reasonable' use of land might be; here a reasonable accommodation could be to permit A to play the piano only at certain times while at other times B could rest; conversely, B could not rest at all times were this to keep A from his music entirely. This solution would restrict an otherwise free use of premises; A's right to play and B's to rest would now be confined to times or periods when most people normally play or rest in their homes. Suppose, however, that A and B reject this compromise; suppose that B requires longer rests or that A cannot give up the piano as he earns his living as a pianist. In such a conflict of interests something else will have to give: either A has to limit his interest in earning his living, or B has to take less care of himself. However, and this is now the interesting difficulty, how are we to decide what or whose sacrifice this should be;

we have no independent standard by which the respective interests can be assessed; if anything they seem of equal worth. To avoid this deadlock we have to consider the situation from another point of view external to A's and B's own personal wants. More particularly, we now have to begin to ask questions like these: how would a decision in favour of A or in favour of B affect third parties; which decision would be less likely to affect either's family; what, more broadly, would be 'better' for society: should we accord a preference to those earning a living, or should we protect the sick. Clearly a great deal will depend on our utilitarian perceptions of the relevant social consequences at any given time or place as well as how desirable or otherwise we view certain states of affairs: all of which are obviously considerations of a 'public' character as they transcend purely 'personal' interests.

Whatever the decision, the party losing out will have to sacrifice at any rate some private rights for the sake of a public good. Take a recent court case which shows admirably how far the public interest can go.[11] Villagers had been playing cricket for some seventy years on a small ground surrounded by agricultural fields. Later some of these fields were taken over by developers, houses were built, one of which was bought by the plaintiffs whose rear garden had a boundary with the cricket ground. Inevitably some balls hit beyond the boundary would fall into the garden or onto or against the house. There was no question that if and when this happened the cricket club would be legally liable for any actual damage caused to person or property; the only question was whether, as the plaintiffs demanded, the cricket club should cease playing altogether, seeing that this caused considerable inconvenience and interference with the enjoyment of their property; at the very least the plaintiffs could not safely remain in their garden while cricket was played. The court (by a majority) refused to accede to this demand. They saw the dispute as a conflict between the interests of the public and the interest of a private individual; where the latter sought to maintain the privacy of a home and garden, the public interest represented the desires of the village as a whole, including the opportunity of young people to engage in outdoor games; if the cricket club had to stop playing where they did they would have nowhere else to go. However the decision that the club should not be driven out also meant that the plaintiffs had to sacrifice or to adjust or modify certain of their otherwise fully recognised private rights in favour of a public interest, that of enabling villagers to continue a pastime long enjoyed.

Such utilitarian ideas of public or social interests can have wider application still. Instead of merely depriving a person of a benefit, e.g. that of enjoying his house and garden to the full, we may impose on him a considerable burden, in fact the sort of punitive burden we impose on a person where he has been guilty of inflicting avoidable harm. There are a few, though only a few, such instances in the law, those usually referred to as 'strict' or 'absolute' liability where a person is made legally liable (liable to pay compensation) even where he is obviously without fault or blame in relation to an injury, except that he is, as it happens, not altogether unconnected with the activity that did cause the plaintiff's harm. The most vivid, also the most extreme, example of this is the legal doctrine of vicarious liability under which one may sue a master for his servant's wrong if done within the latter's course or scope of employment. So where A, a pedestrian, is negligently run over by C, driving a car, A may sue not only C for compensation, but also B, C's master or employer. Admittedly, primary liability for A's injury still rests on C who remains liable to reimburse B if it is the latter who (usually) is sued by A. But this does not concern A; for whether or not C is in a position to reimburse B, the point of the present rule is precisely to shift the risk of C's lack of means to B. If B is thus legally liable to A, what is the moral basis on which this liability rests? Observe again what the moral problem is. B has done nothing to cause the injury except to employ C, but this, by itself, is not a culpable act.

Nor, as we suppose, has C done anything to indicate that he is not a careful driver; he may have acquitted himself admirably of special or additional tests, specially instituted by B, so that B cannot be blamed on the score of putting dangerous drivers on the road. In short, B has done nothing, in terms of an avoidable or responsible action, to bring about A's injury; one definitely cannot assert that B acted 'unjustly' towards A.

Are we then to say that legal rules have their own separate origins, that to this extent law and morals have to be kept apart? Such an answer would be quite unsatisfactory as it would deny the very possibility of morally criticising or justifying legal rules. Nor is such moral escapism here really necessary since it is far from impossible to suggest a moral basis for B's liability. Indeed the difficulty of finding such a basis only arises because we tend to seek it through a notion of justice as applied against B; the position, as we shall now see, is much simpler if considered from a utilitarian point of view. From this side it does appear 'wrong' or, in a broader sense, even 'unjust' or 'unfair' that A might be left injured yet without effective redress, if (as we suppose) C happens to be financially useless to A. This being the case, it is not absurd to say that as between A and B and C, C being B's man, A should have an action against B; not, to be sure, on the ground that B has done or caused harm to A, only that it is a socially 'better' or 'fairer' distribution of burdens if B were to carry some financial liability for a state of affairs that includes the fact that A's injury has been made more likely by an activity after all initiated by B; not to mention the further fact that the person actually causing the harm usually belongs (historically always belonged) to a class of people quite unable to deal with financial disasters of this kind. To hold B liable is then to respond to A's special needs just as it is to acknowledge a public or social interest against leaving a victim like A financially or medically helpless, assuming the absence of accident or other insurance that would otherwise take care of him.

Of course B cannot, even here, be asked to carry this liability unlimitedly; there must still be some connection between him and the injury; hence a major legal limitation is that the servant must act within 'the course of his employment' and not, as the phrase goes, 'on a frolic of his own'. This limitation has given rise to quite a few legal complications, since the criteria of what falls within or without a servant's 'course' of employment are difficult to define; difficult precisely because the principle of vicarious liability, though it puts the legal or financial liability on the employer, does not and cannot also tell him how he can possibly avoid that liability except by not employing servants, which however is not really helpful advice. Indeed all this reveals a particular weakness about public interest and social utility as a moral policy, at any rate in situations of this sort. Certainly the public interest now identified does represent a moral judgement that derives from a utilitarian preference for a state of affairs in which an injured person is more adequately assisted than he might otherwise be. But what this utilitarian approach lacks is the specific limitation possessed by those moral or legal rules that are more particularly based on justice, as these are rules that do not impose liability unless an individual is actually responsible for the harm done if only because he could have avoided doing what he did; a utilitarian approach, concerned as it is with what seems 'best' for everybody, imposes liability regardless of individual responsibility. Nevertheless, as our present legal example shows, this utilitarian approach, too, seeks to limit liability to some extent—here by insisting on a particular nexus as between employer and employee, a limitation which, on further scrutiny, does seem to be once more inspired by notions of justice than by those of utility, as the limitation now in question might in fact be shown to be somewhat disutilitarian in the sense that it diminishes rather than increases total happiness. The result is that we seem again in the presence of a composite form of utilitarianism; utilitarian preferences are combined with as well as qualified by considerations drawn from justice, or at least by considerations inspired by it.

SOME MORAL DILEMMAS

There are, finally, situations for which we have no satisfactory moral answer whatever approach we take, whether through justice or through utility or through a combination of both. These, broadly, are situations where we are confronted with a choice between two evils, or at best between a greater and a lesser evil, the paradigm case being that of the proverbial mariners who shipwrecked and starving decide to slaughter one of their own. There is little or nothing one seems able or willing to say about such a deed: as Freud remarked, one recoils in horror without taking sides.

Even where one does take sides, against the killers (for example), one immediately recognises extenuating facts. In a famous English case a number of seamen, after drifting for about fifteen days in a lifeboat without food or water, discussed the idea of sacrificing one man to save the others, and on the eighteenth day decided to kill the cabin-boy, 17 years old, by now too sick to participate in the discussion of his fate. The seamen were held guilty of murder, clear though it was that the verdict would never be applied; indeed they were soon given a full pardon from the Crown.[12] It is of some interest that the captain, who had been the first to suggest that one would have to be sacrificed, promptly informed the police of what they had done; he was at once arrested, much to his surprise as he expected to be allowed to go home after a full report. The jury, too, was very uncertain as to whether the prisoners were truly guilty of murder, while newspapers confidently predicted that even if held guilty, they would be pardoned in due course. The judges similarly recommended clemency, though they refused to support the proposition that necessity might justify homicide even apart from self-defence. Like everybody else, the judges were torn two ways: between saying, on the one hand, that however great the necessity this did not condone taking another's life; and holding, on the other, that this was not a case for the execution of the death penalty, though sentence of death was duly pronounced.

It will also be clear that such a dilemma cannot be avoided whichever moral view one holds. Occasionally it is suggested that 'justice' or 'utility' may, even in such a case, lead to different results. A utilitarian view, the suggestion is, would not spare the cabin-boy, given a choice between the life of one and the lives of many, whereas 'justice' would certainly have spared the boy whatever the fate of the other mariners: is not this exactly what the maxim *fiat justitia pereat mundus* implies? Still, one may ask whether this maxim can really be taken quite so literally. Does justice really mean that no exception can be made even where the lives of many are at stake? Is it unquestionably 'just' to treat the lives of many just as we treat the life of one? Does this maxim fully represent our attitudes in situations of this kind? And is it really true that utilitarianism quite so unhesitatingly endorses the sacrifice of a human being even where the lives of several are involved, for even a utilitarian may think it far better for society to uphold the sanctity of life in the long run than to make concessions for rare emergencies. Let us look at two other examples of perhaps greater modern actuality.[13] George, a young chemist, very urgently needs a job to feed his wife and small children upon whom the effect of his unemployment is profoundly damaging. The only job available is one in chemical warfare reasearch to which George is strongly opposed, though his wife somewhat less so. Next, Jim chancing to be somewhere in South America where twenty Indians are about to be shot as political hostages is told by Pedro, the chief of the firing squad, that if Jim himself will shoot one Indian the other nineteen will be let off, but if he refuses all twenty will die. What are George and Jim to do? If they believe in justice their dilemma will be complete, but if they are utilitarians, so it is contended, there can be little difficulty since from a utilitarian viewpoint the morally right thing is for George to take the job and for Jim to shoot the Indian. Any bad feelings that George and Jim might have cannot now have great weight; even for Jim such feelings seem somehow irrelevant, seeing that utilitarian calculations are primarily about what is socially at stake, not with what George and Jim may take as their personal 'integrity'. [14]

But the position here seems even more complex. The utilitarian is not 'obviously' on the side of George's taking the job or Jim's shooting the Indian. The reason why George and Jim may eventually do what they do is that when everything is said and their own feelings fully taken into account, this is the only thing they think they can do under the circumstances. To say, for example, that George should not take the job so long as he respects his integrity is to overlook his precise dilemma which is whether his family is starve because he rejects the one position he can get. Even so, one would not confidently blame George were he to refuse the job, no matter how painful for his family; one would even be tempted to admire the steadfast strength of his pacifist beliefs. As for Jim, he may indeed consider himself a utilitarian, yet nevertheless feel the greatest repugnance at taking another man's life, and if he does may regret this to the end of his days though not less convinced that what he did was, given the facts, the only thing he could have done. His dilemma, in other words, is not resolved by his utilitarian views; what he does is, in fact, a 'disutility' he has to weigh against another, perhaps more tempting, 'disutility', that of running away from trying to save nineteen lives *ex hypothesi* savable for the life of one; his moral 'integrity' seems crippled whatever he does. Sometimes, it is true, we do distinguish between greater and smaller misfortunes as we do seem more disturbed by an accident killing (say) nineteen persons than by the death of one. But this is now no real consolation if only because these are events we did not cause, for which therefore we do not hold ourselves responsible, quite unlike Jim's example where he himself is to become responsible for killing one.

These then are dilemmas which do not disappear with a 'correct' moral theory; not even utilitarianism can cure our feelings of moral unease. In fact moral theory here breaks down; not only are our feelings pulling in opposite directions, these are situations in which everyone must make his own decision, indeed a sort of 'existentialist' decision, one which may be right for him but not be (universalisably) right for everyone faced with the same facts.[15] Unlike the earlier examples of the neighbours or the village cricketers where we could resort to an external standard of public interest to resolve deadlocked private interests, in the present cases, especially that of the mariners or that of Jim's predicament, public interest cannot help, precisely because the issue is no longer one of personal hardship or inconvenience but becomes a matter of life and death. If indeed there is a public policy it is that intimated in the cabin-boy's case, namely, that even extreme necessity does not justify the taking of another man's life.

BRIEF RETROSPECT

It is time to draw together some major points. The first is that, in the field of distribution just as elsewhere, we cannot argue rationally on the basis of our private views or intuitions alone. What one person may consider 'just' or 'fair' or 'right', another may see as exactly the opposite; in fact every honest disagreement is largely a difference of intuitive attitudes. The person with whom you disagree may hold what you think eccentric views, but this alone does not dispose of his grievance of being treated wrongly or unjustly in some distribution of the goods of life. To deal fully with such a grievance one needs arguments to show why a complaint either is tenable or is not, which however are arguments that in turn require reasons capable of serving as external standards on the basis of which any one argument can be consistently assessed. But more: since such reasons or standards cannot be only formal, but have to be substantive or material if only to give content to them; since, moreover, those reasons or standards raise considerations of a 'commutative' kind as distinct from considerations pertaining to a person's liberty or immunity, we cannot find our now relevant reasons or standards except in the various distributive options that we actually have — with the proviso that we order these options in a coherent scheme, not only to eliminate possible inconsistencies between them but also to relate each option to a distinctive type-situation which it is, so to speak, representative of.

In this way we can assess our grievances against particular backgrounds of distinguishable reasons and facts. Thus one sort of grievance can be that things have been distributed not in accordance with an agreement express or implied, another grievance that things have been distributed in violation of some cooperative activity either voluntarily undertaken (as joining a team) or required to be observed if the aim is to obtain in rotation a scarce advantage (as joining a queue). In the absence of such 'agreed' or 'cooperative' tests a grievance will have to resort to two other grounds: one, whether one can claim to have made the same or even a greater contribution than another to the stock of still relatively scarce goods, in which case one appeals to the notion of merit or desert; a second, whether one can claim to have an immediate and absolute need for the bare necessities of life, or one can ask for a minor adjustment of an otherwise average (or equal) share, which gives rise to the notion of need. Concomitantly, we will have seen that 'justice' and 'utility', far from basically at odds, often come to the same result, sometimes even complement each other, although in varying ways. In some cases utilitarianism does cast its moral net rather wider than justice, especially where it stresses a public or collective interest. Accordingly, a utilitarian approach can tip the moral balance where individual claims are otherwise deadlocked just as it can deal with situations where justice, emphasising, as it primarily does, individual actions and individual responsibility, cannot morally cope with a doctrine such as that of strict liability, a doctrine called 'strict' precisely because it deals not with culpable or avoidable actions but with unfortunate or undesirable states of affairs. Even here, however, a utilitarian public interest cannot tilt the balance beyond a certain point: it can adjust social or financial advantages for the purpose of some compromise, yet it too cannot punish the innocent, nor condone purely expedient measures if they occasion too great a damage or disadvantage to someone else.

Finally, we may have observed that our distributive grievances, though extremely versatile nevertheless seem to fall into two broad groups. In the first, our grievances do make contact with a notion of harm. Indeed the closer they are to harm, the more specific also the complaint; this is particularly so in the case of extreme physical need where a refusal to help can have fatal effects. The position is somewhat similar with distributive complaints that rest on a particular agreement and its breach, or on the (explicit or implicit) standards either of some agreed cooperative activity or of a selective group; here the relevant advantages or benefits due to each are more or less specified or at least specifiable, so that they create their own measure of expectations which, if disappointed, give rise to a grievance close to a sense of harm, though now of course not physical harm, protective as this is of individual liberty or immunity, but harm of a social or economic kind consisting of an uneven burden or an extra hardship that diminishes expected advantages.[16] In the other group, our distributive grievances have no such close connection with specifiable harm; our grievances now look more like 'open' demands or campaigns for the adoption of more 'fraternal' or charitable or cooperative standards, or for some compromise between private and public interests mainly through political processes. Here, moreover, confronted by a relative scarcity of the goods of life, our grievances draw their force from 'communal' or 'welfaristic' considerations, simply because our grievances now are directed not against individuals but against a whole group or society, being grievances about the existence of general social ills. Such welfare considerations, as we already hinted in Chapter 2, will appeal to our common or collective benevolence even as they, in any case, appeal to our sense of political expediency, to persuade those who are to make the sacrifices or those in control of our resources that, in certain circumstances, there are economic concessions it would be prudent or wise to initiate. And such considerations will also be more persuasive than conclusive, in the sense that they rather belong to the realm of political and prudential morality, not to the more rigorous morality of justice between man and man.

5 Precedents, Principles and Practices

Having examined how a moral judgement is rationally supported, or a moral grievance rationally advanced or met, we turn to moral reasoning more concerned with the orderly development of moral rules, the process by which they gradually accumulate, brick by brick, so to speak, to emerge as moral patterns or practices or as moral customs or codes. Moral reasoning, we shall begin to see, has really two quite distinguishable even if closely interrelated sides to it. The first has to do with moral decisions or judgements, the moral reasons we can and must give for imposing blame, the principal task here being to identify the conditions under which a decision or judgement qualifies as moral and not as of another sort. The second side deals more specifically with moral rules and their logical careers. Since moral judgements are not simply *ad hoc* responses to particular grievances, but are rules about kinds of actions as well as kinds of affairs, every rule, though deriving from a past moral judgement, becomes relevant to future situations as well; future conduct is what a rule is for; indeed just this is the basis for saying that moral rules must treat like cases alike and unlike cases differently, this last for no more recondite reason than that a decision about situation X does not extend to situation Y.

What is more, to make a moral rule is to establish a moral precedent; there is a precedent because the moral rule, connecting as it does the future with the past, thereby limits new decision-making as it withdraws a moral judgement from being made again. For it is of the nature of a moral rule that it commits us to a decision once it is made simply because we cannot decide a like case differently, although the question to what precise extent we are so committed may still need to be settled by further argument. Much the same is true of legal rules or precedents, that is, the precedents emerging from judge-made law which differs from law based on statute or the judicial interpretations of statute. Of course legal precedents must now be taken without their various 'technical' or 'procedural' characteristics; but these anyhow only affect their actual operation, not their basic nature, for the simple reason that the lawyer's doctrine of precedent is, in substance, equally about applying past judgements to future cases if they are similar. Unless the lawyer recognised such a doctrine, unless he observed the requirement of 'following' an earlier decision or case, there would be no common law and no case-law: there would be cases, but no law, no principles or rules, since a judge would decide each case irrespective of other decisions, however similar, just as his own decision would be irrelevant for any future reference. In English law this truth was grasped, almost instinctively, virtually from the very start: new cases, it was said as early as the thirteenth century, should be adjudged in like manner, proceeding *a similibus ad similia*.[1]

Indeed, the lawyer's technique of precedent is an apt working demonstration of universalisability which an earlier chapter discussed at length. For just as, as we then saw, the logical purpose of universalisability is to enable us to argue morally in terms of rules, so the doctrine of precedent is designed to help us translate a particular decision into a more general principle. To make a previous decision 'followable', to convert it into an 'applicable' precedent, the common lawyer accordingly distinguishes between the *ratio decidendi* of a case and its *obiter dicta*, the latter being judicial observations regarded as rather 'by the way'. As the term *ratio decidendi* suggests, a judgement must contain a reason for a decision, that is, a reason that though related to also transcends the particular facts of the case; hence a reason that takes the form of, or is at least translatable or expandable into, a wider *ratio* or rule. Admittedly not every judgement bequeaths a clear reason or principle; a judge may give more reasons than necessary, may give different reasons, or confused or unclear ones, or reasons which are 'too wide', or the judge may (though this happens rarely) give virtually no reasons at all. But overlooking these problems, the point to stress is that a later court can only 'follow' or 'apply' a given precedent if it can know, or discover, or sometimes re-construct the so-called *ratio* of the previous case.

Furthermore, to extract or formulate a *ratio* the lawyer becomes involved in a very selective as well as 'generalising' exercise. As he cannot rely on *all* the facts of the previous case, he has to select those facts or features in it that may be relevant for the new case. Yet how can this selection proceed? Only, it should now be obvious, by knowing or appreciating the moral point or purpose behind the previous case. Suppose that a big red-headed man is found guilty of deliberately injuring a smaller dark-haired man on a Sunday afternoon. We immediately understand that quite a few facts (red-headed, dark-haired, big, small, Sunday afternoon) have to be discarded as being morally irrelevant; they are irrelevant facts or attributes because they do not relate to, let alone identify, the action or grievance which the case is morally about. So the fact that the harm was done on a Sunday by a red-headed man is immaterial to the injury; to regard it as a material fact would thus be to commit what is known as the 'non-cause' (*non causa pro causa*) fallacy; it would also mean that we could have a moral grievance about somebody being big or small, red- or dark-haired, and so on.[2]

Unless, again, we appreciate the moral import of the earlier case, there is no way of assessing the relevant similarities or differences between the previous case and the new. What does make two cases similar is not just the facts that look similar, for they may not so appear; two cases, not identical, can always look more or less similar or more or less different. There are cases in which the factual similarities appear great, yet the legal (and moral) differences are not significant, just as, correspondingly, there are cases in which the factual similarities seem small yet the legal or moral difference is considerable. Nor can we say whether two cases are materially similar or different by suggesting that (respectively) the same or different legal rule applies, for we do not know whether the same or different rules do apply until we have first determined the strength of the similarity or the difference of the cases. At all events, since the relevant similarities or differences here are neither self-evident nor ostensive (unlike a difference, say, between blue and red), they become determinable only in the light of a particular moral point. Without such a moral point, we would not even know which similarities or differences to consider as relevant, nor know, even in outline, what ('similar' or 'different') questions to ask so as to evaluate the facts of the case: the search for similarity or difference would be like the blind seeking the blind.

We begin to see that legal precedents involve reasoning that greatly overlaps with moral reasoning, at any rate over a wide central area now of interest to us. This is not to deny that there are other areas which show no such overlap, where legal reasoning does indeed go its own way; but this (as we shall see more fully in Chapter 6) is mainly so in borderline cases which do not affect the present argument. Indeed it needs particular emphasis that legal reasoning would not only become a somewhat vacuous exercise were it insensitive to the moral features that determine the relevant similarities or differences, the moral-legal overlap we have adverted to throws light on moral rules or precedents as well; it shows that moral rules, too, must be firm and settled if they are to be applicable to future (similar) cases, if they are thus to perform the function of rules. In other words, what is sometimes called the 'binding' nature of precedents is not just a feature of the legal doctrine of precedents; the same feature has to be present in the moral realm: the whole idea of reasoning by way of similarity and difference could not take a firm grip unless previous precedents (or judgements or rules or principles) had this 'binding' force, i.e. the force to commit future decisions on the basis of old.[3]

What then of the familiar claim that legal reasoning represents an instance of reasoning by analogy, this being taken as a self-sufficient kind of reasoning. Certainly the law reports are replete with cases which are either an analogous extension or a disanalogous qualification of previous ones. A spectacular example is a relatively recent line of decisions which analogously adapted case after case, so that what began as a somewhat limited rule ended up as a wide and comprehensive principle. A manufacturer of ginger-ale (to tell as briefly as possible a rather hackneyed tale) was held liable for the injury his defective product caused to an ultimate consumer, many steps removed from the manufacturer, the product reaching that consumer without any possibility of intermediate inspection as it was marketed in a sealed and opaque container.[4] This liability, initially very narrow, was however soon extended in two ways: to defendants who were not manufacturers but intermediaries like dealers, then to articles which might reach a consumer with at least some possibility, if not a probability, of intermediate inspection. The details of this are not here important, except to observe that cumulative analogies eventually produced a principle imposing liability for any injury-prone article whose harmful defect is not patently obvious. Still, to say that all this exemplifies, as it admittedly does, reasoning by analogy is not to say very much. For to say this, and no more, leaves out the crucial point that even reasoning by analogy requires a criterion by virtue of which an analogy is found or, for that matter, a disanalogy recognised. What is worse, it leaves out the crucial point that what carries the analogy forward and keeps it on its proper path is the moral principle of avoidable harm; the legal spute in these cases is always about some injury or disadvantage which a responsible human agent could with some care or foresight have avoided.

Indeed to say that legal reasoning is simply reasoning by analogy can lead to even deeper misconceptions; one is the assertion that the perception of the relevant analogies or disanalogies here is purely psychological; another is the misleading controversy as to whether a judge is to see the *ratio decidendi* of an earlier case 'through his own eyes' or through those of the earlier decider, one theorist suggesting that the relevant eyes are those of the earlier judge, since we have first to determine the earlier *ratio* before we can apply it, while according to another theory the relevant eyes are the subsequent judge's since it is he who now has to make the decision, so that the *ratio* of the earlier judge becomes mere *dictum*.[5] A little reflection shows that neither theory is very satisfactory. The former leads in fact to a very restricted view of applying a previous decision (rather resembling the literal interpretation of a statute) which can only with difficulty be called reasoning by analogy; for if the new case is to be decided through the eyes of the earlier judge, we would be (deductively) giving effect to what that judge already envisaged; hence we would be recapitulating the old decision rather than extending it analogously. The latter theory, if strictly or faithfully applied, would virtually require each subsequent judge to announce a new principle: a principle which, no doubt, would incorporate the earlier result but which would not necessarily bear any resemblance to the antecedent principle, which, again, would hardly add up to analogous reasoning; at best we would now (intuitively) connect legal results rather than reason about them in the light of a common or general (moral-legal) principle. Both theories, in other words, regard a precedent as a sort of positive datum or source of law, so that if you adhere to that source, as (positivistically) you must, the consequence is either that you see the earlier decision 'through its own eyes' (as the first theory suggests), or you transfer the positive force to the subsequent decision regarding the earlier to be mere dictum (as the second theory recommends).

What these and similar theories so much obscure is that the strength of a precedent does not reside in its being a legal source like a statute but in its being the starting or serial point in a chain of reasoning about or around a common rule or principle. Or, speaking more broadly, the true significance of precedent is better seen through the eyes not of a positivist but of a natural lawyer. In practice, indeed, lawyers do argue, most of the time, like natural lawyers when they argue about *pros* and *cons* or about the 'merits' of a case, or about their analogous extensions or disanalogous qualifications. Lawyers so argue instinctively, because there is no other way, not because they know that this is, theoretically, the right way to go about things. It is true that there are many situations in which an earlier decision does have a sort of controlling force, almost like a statute; but here lawyers no longer argue about the merits of a case but more about formal consistency; these are cases, as already mentioned and as we shall further explain in the next chapter, which happen to be so much on the borderline as to make a new *pro* or *con* decision either very difficult or pointless, since morally it no longer matters whether the new decision goes one way or the other. And in these situations a judge cannot decide a case, though decide he still must, except by what may be called a purely 'categorial' approach, the judge now merely trying to fit the case into its nearest conceptual pigeon-hole, an approach which in time will even produce what is known as 'technical' law or 'legal conceptualism'. It may equally be true that, as a matter of practice, such 'technical' precedents outnumber those with a moral content. Even so, it should now be clearer that it is moral precedents that form both the initial basis and the forward thrust of legal development.

PRINCIPLES AND EXCEPTIONS

An outstanding feature of normative (moral as well as legal) rules is that they are susceptible to, in fact even encourage, exceptions, quite unlike scientific or technical principles which describe or picture the world as it is, so that an exception would directly and falsifiably challenge this picture—unless the so-called exception were merely a way for saying 'some' instead of 'all' or 'probably' instead of 'always'. In moral or legal discourse, however, rules or principles are not similarly 'absolute' but are 'qualifiable' or merely *prima facie* statements, thus always open to exceptions, this for the simple and familiar reason that normative rules contain both descriptive and evaluative elements: a descriptive element because rules cannot prescribe conduct unless they indicate what, in terms of actions or events, that conduct is to consist of; an evaluative element because both moral and legal rules are primarily meant to guide human conduct according to what are, ultimately, our shared values and sympathies. All this also explains why in applying moral or legal precedents we have to deal with two levels of similarity and difference, a descriptive and evaluative level; hence why it is (a feature we adverted to earlier) that even a close descriptive similarity between two cases may disclose a significant moral difference, while close moral affinities may cover what may look like wide factual divergencies.

Obviously the exceptions we are now speaking of are not grammatical qualifications merely limiting the descriptive scope of a principle by confining it to a particular place or time ('No Smoking except in the smoking room', No Parking except after 5 p.m.'); rather are they exceptions which operate like evaluative counter-principles. So while the principle may prescribe responsibility for an action, the exception or counter-principle may qualify it by introducing a special excuse or defence to meet special circumstances. The exception may be no less general than the principle it limits, as it may itself derive from a wider moral reason such as the reason that since 'ought implies can', one only ought (or ought not) to do things which an agent can actually help doing (or not doing). We say, for example, that a promisor ought to keep his promise except where there is an impossibility of performance such as death or sickness, or some other *force majeure* making performance not merely inconvenient but impossible. Or we may have a general rule like 'do not speak defamatory words of others' which is then subjected to such exceptions as truth or privilege or fair comment, all of them defences designed to give effect to a countervailing principle of free speech or truthful reporting even at the cost of the person defamed.

This exception-making process may go even further. What begins as a 'principle' may become an 'exception', while the erstwhile 'exception' may turn into the 'principle', the offshoot now virtually becoming the parent. There is nothing very surprising about this reversal. As the 'exception' is no less of a 'principle' than the principle *stricto sensu*, subsequent precedents may introduce so many exceptions as to give them far greater practical import than still retained by the principle, so much so that it may even appear logically more convenient (using the word 'logical' now in an expository sense) to put the original principle as the exception, and to make the exceptions into the basic principle, thus switching their order of sequence for purposes of clearer presentation. Here as before we then see principle and counter-principle in direct confrontation as they go in opposite directions, yet nevertheless still dependent on each other, inviting mutual comments including reasons and counter-reasons, the principle in terms of the counter-principle, the counter-principle in terms of the principle. This does not mean that even if we decide that in a particular case there is no duty to keep one's promise because that promise falls within the exception or counter-principle, we thereby change our moral view or moral rule that normally one ought to keep one's promise. On the contrary, to argue for an exception to a principle is to unpack and thus to highlight the latter's essential purpose, and so to strengthen its original or residual justification. This perhaps explains why the phrase 'the exception proves the rule' is not a nonsense; what the exception does is to 'prove' the rationale of the rule as now viewed from a sharper perspective.

It is important to realise that this evaluative element diminishes but never altogether disappears even in what become established or settled moral notions. To see this better let us briefly compare the formation of a moral concept such as 'murder' with that of such eminently descriptive notions as 'red' or 'table'. As regards these latter, it is at once clear that we define colour words differently from object words. When we look at something described as 'red', we recognise a quality (redness), so to speak, in its own right, it being possible for two objects to be different only in their colour (one red, the other not), though otherwise identical. When we look at other objects, their material qualities, one quickly realises, are capable of varying so widely (a table, for example, can be round or square, large or small, three- or four-legged, and so on) that the qualities are not exhaustively enumerable since we can always find new makes of tables; no definition of table can therefore be derived solely from its material qualities, quite unlike a colour word the definition of which is exclusively entailed by its colour-property. It follows that we cannot define 'table' except by identifying its *formal* attributes, attributes that will now have to fasten on the conventional use or purpose of tables, in particular their flat surface elevated at a certain height at which normal people can sit; obviously we need, and accordingly make, pieces of furniture to sit at, and it is just this facility which furnishes the criterion enabling us to pick out among different objects those that do and those that do not qualify as tables. One would not describe a ten-foot high contraption as having 'tableness', nor perhaps a foot-stool, even though the former may serve as a table for giants to sit at, the latter for dwarfs. [6]

Turning to moral concepts we see that these display a similar lack of entailment between their definability and their material elements. In the case of 'murder', to take a simple example, the material elements include many possible events: poisoning, shooting, stabbing and endless other homicidal acts. Like an object word, definability will therefore have to be found in a formal element. Nor is this element far to seek, for we can find it in the lawyerly definition of murder: 'taking a person's life with malice aforethought'. Not that this is the end of the story. Though, in ordinary language, the legal definition would certainly include many, it does not include all possible, instances of murder. Thus A may 'take' B's life even with 'malice aforethought', yet act as an executioner, or in war, or in self-defence which we may regard (and lawyers do regard) as cases of justifiable homicide; or A may 'take' B's life again with 'malice' but in circumstances which somehow diminish or deny his responsibility, as where he acts under provocation, or in a *crime passionel*. The point of all this is that our definition of murder does not include but rather leaves open the possibility of our disagreeing, in a situation not yet covered by rules, whether a particular homicide is to qualify as murder or not—a disagreement, moreover, which is quite different from whether or not an object is to be called a 'table'. Here the disagreement is about the use of words, also one that is relatively easily resolved, provided we agree, as we normally do, to recognise the same difference between pieces of furniture that are, and are not, sittable at. In the case of murder, however, our disagreement is not solely about the language we speak, it is no less about our attitudes to very serious, indeed fatal, injury; about how we evaluate that injury in the given but (as yet) untried circumstances in which it occurred; whether we are to ascribe to it the degree of blame and responsibility we usually attach to deliberate homicide.[7]

To concede that moral (or, for that matter, corresponding legal) rules retain a crucial evaluative element is by no means to stumble into the trap of emotivism or subjectivism which of course would make moral reasoning impossible. For this evaluative element is itself caught and controlled by a number of conditions (some of which have already been adverted to) which here keep our evaluations on a straight though not necessarily also on a narrow path. As these

evaluations have to be universalised to make them part of a
rule or precedent, they cannot be evaluative in a purely
personal or subjective sense, but have to be evaluative about
kinds of actions or states of affairs; and as such evaluations
must be such as to lend themselves to moral argument, they
will have to advance reasons such as, most typically, reasons
having to do with avoidable harm. It is true that the notion of
harm, resting as it ultimately does, on a commonly and
vicariously shared value-judgement, is not a notion that is
conceptually very precise; but it is none the worse for that as
it can still function as a norm or standard. Wittgenstein, it
may be remembered, did not share Frege's view that a
blurred concept is not a concept or that an area with vague
boundaries cannot be called an area.[8] He thought it definitely
not true that vague concepts are somehow useless, for they
can serve as sign-posts, as 'avoidable harm' does here, that
give us a clear enough sense of direction as to an area of
conduct we morally wish to proscribe.

Our evaluative element is controlled by yet another
feature. This is that in many cases the need to evaluate or
reevaluate new situations turns out to be greatly diminished,
depending on the descriptive strength of the formal definition. For the wider the latter's descriptive scope, the
greater will be its field of included similarities or excluded
differences. So even though the formal or defining element of
a moral concept can never insulate it altogether from
evaluation, the fact remains that a formal definition may offer
much conceptual stability. For one thing, the formal definition of murder can stand by itself, notwithstanding the
fact that as a principle murder is subject to old and possibly
new exceptions; for these exceptions can relate to circumstances which are sufficiently separable so as not to challenge
directly the main formal definitions. For another thing, as we
have already seen, even a formal definition can have wide
material applicability, if only because, as in the example of
murder, it does not in the least matter how, or in which of
many possible ways, the killing occurs: whether by shooting

or poisoning, stabbing or bashing; to formulate a rule like 'do not deliberately kill' thus covers all the possibilities of homicide without having to enumerate all its means or methods. The reason why this is so stems from the fact that we are dealing with deliberate actions, that is, actions avoidable *par excellence*; as clearly avoidable actions they are also the most amenable to regulation: we can formulate rules which though general do not forfeit their action-specificity.

The position is very different in relation to non–deliberate injury. Consider a rule like 'do not negligently or carelessly injure another'. Negligent or careless actions are, by definition, unintended and undesired. Still, in manifestly dangerous situations (say, driving too fast, playing with dynamite) the rule seems both clear and sufficient. In other situations, less patently dangerous or reckless, such a rule becomes however utterly indefinite in terms of action-guidance; indefinite because there is no specific action the rule enjoins us to do or to forbear from; one cannot even begin to be careful unless one also knows what to be careful about. The difficulty is even greater in situations bordering on pure accident. A legal case offers an excellent illustration. While unloading a ship, one of the stevedores dropped a plank; the plank, hitting something, touched off a spark which ignited oil vapour in the hold, which put the ship aflame; the stevedores were held liable in negligence for the whole damage. [9] We need not discuss the decision as such; what concerns us more is the virtual impossibility of devising satisfactory rules for such a situation. To say (e.g.) 'do not drop planks setting off sparks in vaporous places', though seemingly hitting the root of the trouble, far from covers the situation entirely. The planks might slip rather than be dropped because of a stevedore's slippery shoes or any number of other contingencies one cannot even think of, let alone list exhaustively.

This, too, is why, unable to name beforehand the specific action we want to see avoided yet still disposed to ascribe

responsibility, we have to say (what in fact lawyers have been
saying), namely, that the defendant was 'negligent' or 'at
fault' in causing damage which, if not actually foreseen, was
nevertheless foreseeable with ordinary knowledge or prudence. To speak of 'foreseeability' is clearly designed to make
contact with avoidability, to suggest that the defendant could
have avoided doing what he did, could have acted more
responsibly, so that (in other words) he is not now being held
'strictly' liable. Nevertheless what 'foreseeable' here means in
terms of concrete actions or precautions is often left rather
vague and unspecified: which is to say that concepts like
'forseeable' or 'negligent' are now used 'defeasibly' in the
sense that there is no descriptive formula capable of covering
all the conditions under which an unintended consequence
will be deemed to be 'negligently' caused or 'reasonably
foreseeable' for the purpose of ascribing responsibility.[10]

PATTERNS AND PRACTICES

Where moral concepts are defeasible, or where there are
relatively few moral or legal precedents in a given
area, evaluation will play an important part in decision-
making since we shall need to translate our somewhat
abstract moral norm against harm into more concrete
decisions. However as such decisions, together with their
corresponding rules and precedents, accumulate, as accumulate they must so long as we treat similar cases similarly,
a particular area of moral conduct will acquire ever more
descriptive and more detailed content. The accumulating
detail will indeed begin to form a conceptual pattern,
forming or clustering either around a typical or frequent type
of harmful action such as 'murder' or 'theft' or 'trespass', or
around certain social roles such as 'father' or 'husband' and so
on. Moreover, the denser and more detailed that pattern, the
more important also the descriptive element as this in fact
now pushes aside the need for constant moral evaluation. In a

manner of speaking, cumulative evaluation even leads to description; it leads to it since what the evaluation, once it has done its work, leaves behind is a result describing certain events or actions now adjudged as morally blameworthy. Or, putting this in another way, once evaluation fills up an area of conduct with a pattern of principles and exceptions, description (or the material or descriptive element of the rules) begins to take over. For similarities and differences now become more guidable by facts (or similarities to facts), if only because we are increasingly able to tell from the facts alone whether and to what extent they are morally significant for the simple reason, as already indicated, that these facts not only describe certain actions, they also convey or encapsulate our moral reactions or attitudes to them. Even more: our moral notions now even seem to assume the character of natural facts, so much so as to make it appear as though certain moral characteristics belonged inherently or intrinsically to certain actions or roles, as though moral rules were socially predetermined, belonging to or deriving from established social practices.[11]

This 'institutional' view has unfortunately tended to obscure the nature of moral practices. Now many an activity can be regarded as a social (as distinct from a specifically moral) practice, provided it occurs with some frequency or regularity or with some social acceptance: weddings or funerals are such practices, just as are games or concerts in our culture. More broadly, we have a practice or institution wherever a complex social activity is governed by a set or 'system' of rules. Another interesting feature here is that the rules relating to the practice have to be, at any rate for the most part, positive or commissive rather than negative or omissive; it does not even seem possible to imagine a practice consisting of purely negative or omissive acts. And this may be an additional reason why practices often appear as typically descriptive; the rules that tell us, for example, how to get married or how to transfer property seem exactly like the rules of chess or the rules instructing us how to make bread. Yet it is just these appearances that can greatly mislead. It is true that the relevant rules in a practice are positive in the sense of being constitutive: the rules of chess tell us how to play chess just as those relating to marriage and property inform us how we validly get married or validly make property transfers. However a crucial difference between these rules surely is that where the rules of chess are autonomously constitutive, the rules about property are heteronomously constitutive in the sense that even as constitutive rules they are not independent of but are dependent or parasitic on regulative rules. Thus the institution of 'property' depends on or assumes the existence of a number of heteronomously regulative rules, in particular rules which require us to refrain from interfering with things held by another person, unless it be with the latter's consent expressed in certain ways. Where, in other words, regulative rules safeguard the property in one proprietor, constitutive rules tell us how such property can be transferred consensually from one person to another, whether by way of sale or gift or testamentary disposition. So a testamentary transfer has to comply with various constitutive rules, namely, that the testator's last will has to be made in writing, signed and attested to by several witnesses; unless these rules are complied with the testamentary disposition will fail because lacking validity.

The fact remains that for all their constitutive super-structure many practices, not just those of making wills but many others as well, cannot be fully understood unless their strictly regulative foundations are kept in mind. So it would be pointless to try to transfer property by a document like a will if property were not a regulatively protected institution. Even a practice like making wills does not then arise completely 'voluntarily'; its regulative foundations puts it apart from such other practices as carrying umbrellas or playing games. Indeed not to see this regulative aspect is to overlook the primary regulative basis of moral, let alone legal, rules: to overlook, that is, that moral and legal rules begin as regulations before they emerge as practices. A good illustration of this is the case of promise-keeping. We turn to consider this in some detail now.

THE PRACTICE OF PROMISE-KEEPING

If we ask why promises are (to be) kept, one frequent philosophical answer now is essentially this: that promising being a practice, to make a promise is therefore to put oneself under an obligation, thereby accepting or confirming an already existing set of rules that make up the practice of promising, of which one rule specifies what it is to promise while another demands its keeping or performing: to promise is thus to promise to keep it, just as to play chess is to proceed to play it according to its rules. On this view, an 'obligation' to keep promises has little or nothing to do with a moral rule directed against avoidable harm; the obligation rather springs from uttering the word 'promise' since, as J. L. Austin suggested, there is a sort of entailment between 'I promise' and 'I ought', so that to say 'I promise' but not to perform the promise is parallel to saying both 'it is' and 'it is not'.[12]

All this is not very satisfactory. To be told that a promise is itself obligatory gives us no way of distinguishing moral from immoral promises which latter, it would be agreed, ought not to be kept. A promise like 'I'll get you' does not mean that I ought to do harm to another though I promised to do it. Also, as Prichard has shown, the notion of a promissory obligation is an extremely odd one.[13] Since in promising all the promisor does is to make certain verbal noises, how can this fact render him bound to perform what he promised? It cannot be that he merely performs his promise because this is wise or useful to do, or because he does not wish to run the risk of never being trusted again; these reasons offer merely prudential, not really moral, considerations. Nor can it be that our sense of obligation lies in, or at any rate presupposes, a prior general agreement among men to keep promises: first, because such an agreement would in turn require a prior agreement supplying the reason why the subsequent agreement should be kept, so leading to an infinite regress; secondly, and more basically, because to presuppose such a prior agreement is tacitly to take for granted what we are required to show; in particular, to take for granted that we are the human beings we already are, i.e. beings thinking themselves bound by an agreement.[14]

The obvious inadequacy of the 'obligatory' approach has led philosophers to look more closely at the concept of a promise, including the promisor's statement of intention, especially his intention to assure the promisee that he will definitely perform what he promised to do. In making a promise A is not just saying he intends to perform but that he *will* perform; A, for example, cannot say 'I intend not to be late, but I may be late'; what he has to say is that he *firmly* intends to be there, so withdrawing his option to be late. This assurance is of importance to the promisee since the promise is for his sake or benefit. Accordingly, to say 'I promise to get you if you don't play' is not a promise but a threat. Accordingly, again, a promise has to be an accepted or acceptable statement of intention, not something the promisee rejects or is utterly indifferent about. To be capable of creating a reliable assurance or expectation the promise must then be of a certain kind: it must not be a patently illusory or impossible promise or a trivial or jocular one. However, to recognise all these conditions still does not answer the question why a promise should be kept; nevertheless, to know what a promise conceptually includes or implies can prove very useful since to know why a promise means what it means can provide certain clues as to its moral nature.

Suppose, for example, A says to B: 'I'll meet you for lunch tomorrow'. Suppose A does not then appear, though B does. Clearly B can now make a complaint, or rebuke A for not excusing himself in advance or not apologising after the event. Why has B a grievance against A? Because he has suffered an inconvenience or disappointment or disadvantage, suffered some harm in the broadest sense, also some harm directly caused by A. At the very least B has a 'right' to complain because, having reasonably counted on A, he (B) was let down, or made to waste his time, or to forego other luncheon arrangements with persons more reliable than A. It is this element of hurt or harm, a sort of insult to B, that calls for A's becoming answerable in the sense that B has a justified censure or complaint, that B can justifiably demand an explanation from A. Of course if B does not really care whether A turns up for lunch, B's complaint will be weak as A will be entitled to say that B did not really count on him. Conversely if B's disappointment is palpably severe as where he suffers substantial financial harm, his complaint will have that much greater force. A promise, in other words, can by its breach inflict financial harm or it can cause only a disappointment but one still grave enough to give rise to a distinctive dialogue of grievances and excuses between the parties concerned. Hence a major reason why we here wish to examine the *concept* of promising, why we want to be clear about what constitutes a proper promise and not something else, seems to be simply this: that the wrong now in question can only be caused by a particular verbal act (A cannot arouse B's expectation unless he not only *says* something to him but says something to him in a particular way); what he says is a verbal act which the word 'promise' now stereotypes.

Of course the essential thing is not what a promise is called but whether as a statement it is not only expectation-creative but also capable of causing personal harm. Hence in distinguishing promises from threats, or mere resolutions, or predictions, we are not so much making a neutral dictionary entry as, rather, relating the promissory words to a standard, now a moral standard, simply because without such a standard it would in fact not be possible to control the various distinctions between promissory statements of intention and other statements of intention not amounting to promises.

What gives these distinctions a point and purpose is that they work out the related conditions of avoidable harm in a particular area of conduct, that of disappointed expectations caused by another's verbal acts. Indeed such an analysis of the moral (and legal) concept of promise supports two concomitant theses this chapter has been so much concerned with: first, that precedents cannot proceed from like to like unless they are kept together by a basic moral theme that includes similarities but excludes differences; and second, that moral concepts are formed as and when accumulating precedents build up a coherent pattern of decisions and distinctions in relation to actions which, though they crowd ·into one descriptive area because of their physical resemblance, yet still need to be sorted out according to one evaluative standard.

It may be objected that the above account, with its special emphasis on avoidable harm, does not, and indeed cannot, satisfactorily deal with situations where no harm to the promisee can be shown: as where (i) A promises to do something for B but B forgets, or where (ii) A makes his promise on B's death-bed, so that B may be no longer around to voice his complaints should A break his promise. In both (i) and (ii) A is still said to be under an obligation to keep his promise, even though there are no discernible ill-effects on B. But neither example is quite so conclusive as may seem at first sight. Taking (ii) first, there is here not much greater difficulty in finding the harm done than finding the harm done to a person killed or murdered by A; as we saw in Chapter 3, our moral rule is a social one, not divorced from the reaction of a group or community as it is not solely an individual but also a vicarious response. As for (i), there are two possibilities: the promisee may have forgotten the promise simply because it matters little or nothing to him, in which case the harm done may be too trivial to be fussed about by the rest of us; or B may have forgotten about the promise being too ill or incapacitated; here the group may vicariously judge the harm to B no less easily than if B had died or were otherwise incapable of making his own complaint to A or to society.

What we have said is not purely a 'consequentialist' or 'utilitarian' account of promise-keeping, or if it is it would be an expanded account. A strictly consequentialist account would (on some utilitarian views) have difficulty with the case where A is excused from keeping a promise because of personal impossibility, even though its breach causes injury to B. If A dies or becomes sick he is unable to do what he promised he would, just as there are other situations of *force majeure* in which we think it just or fair to terminate, or at least modify or suspend, A's duty to B. These situations vividly show the need to consider a promise from the point of view of both sides, the promisor and the promisee, since in evaluating the gravity of the broken promise we have to consider not just the harm to the promisee but also the position of the promisor, namely how able or willing he is to avoid the harm to the promisee especially if the harm is significant. And in these situations a moral calculus of avoidable harm has a great deal of work to do; not so much where the unavoidability is clear (as in death), but where the avoidability of harm itself is arguable: the greater the harm to B, the greater (it may be contended) ought to be the effort to perform; the smaller, correspondingly, should be the scope of *force majeure* apart from extreme impossibilities. This and other problems show why promise-keeping turns into something of a paradigm not only of moral but also of legal reasoning. It directs attention to the moral reasons that lie behind the law of promises (or the law of contract), including the reasons that may support an excuse for a failure to perform. So a judge, unless merely applying clearly settled law, will be involved in moral reasoning wherever he has to decide why a given promise ought to be kept or why its performance may be excused or modified.

It is this bilateral feature of promise-keeping that so markedly differentiates it from the obligation of telling the truth. According to one theory, however, truth-telling is what promise-keeping is essentially reducible to. In making a promise, it has been maintained, A is not so much giving an assurance as making a prediction, this by stating his present intention that something, some act, will be the case; further it is a strong prediction, for by saying 'I will' do this I am not stating anything beyond my control; I am predicting something entirely within my capabilities, something entirely 'up to me', so that if having made this prediction, I do not try to make what I promised the case, I can be blamed for upsetting or falsifying this prediction, for (so to speak) bringing about an untruth.[15] Nevertheless, to see promise-keeping as part of a 'requirement of veracity' does not really advance things. It is true that lying and false promises constitute the same sort of deliberate deception, and it is also true that we can, even in respect of promises, speak of 'prediction' instead of the more usual 'statement of intention'. But this is a substitution of no real significance. If the statement 'I will do' is read as a *firm* intention, it does not matter whether it is a prediction also; and if the statement is not so readable, then 'I will do', though in a sense still predictive, is not predictive enough to give the promisee the assurance he can rely on, a circumstance which would disqualify it as a proper promise.

Even worse, to equate promise-keeping with truth-telling causes us to overlook some more substantial differences between them. A major difference is that a promise allows for a change in the promisor's position as between the time of the promise and the time performance is due. Consider the simple example of a promise by A to look after B's cat while the latter is away for a few days. How does it help in *this* sort of case to resort to a requirement of truth? Suppose that A's promise to look after B's cat was honest or sincere when given, only that he changed his mind because (let us assume) he found looking after B's cat an inconvenience or an imposition, or because he had to change his original intention when unexpectedly called upon to attend a funeral, or see a doctor, and so on. The latter circumstances surely offer a real excuse; and even where A repudiates his promise only because he wants to shed an inconvenient burden, perhaps one too hastily or generously assumed, this too is hardly tantamount to mendacity. The central point however is that whereas the morality of promise-keeping is open to appropriate excuses, no comparable excuses attach to truth-telling, virtually no real excuses at all, except in the case of what we sometimes call 'white' lies, as when I falsely tell B that my name is Tom Smith, which may be utterly immaterial to him, or I tell an incurably sick man that there is still hope so as not to upset his last days. Still excusable lies are very different from excusable promises, for lies are excusable only if they cause no harm while promises can be excused in the interests solely of the promisor, even if a breach results in loss to the promisee. The distinctiveness of promise-keeping has thus a great deal to do with the excuses applying to it.

OBLIGATIONS AND OUGHTS

Our discussion of promises leads to some wider thoughts. We often speak of an obligation to keep promises, as though 'obligation' possessed a special sense. Now, generally, to say someone has an obligation is to say that he ought to do or forbear; accordingly, to speak of an obligation to keep one's promise is simply like saying that one ought to keep a promise; it is the same moral ought that springs from what we have seen to be the promisor's answerability to the promisee for the expectation caused by the promise together with the harm done by its breach. This answerability, we have also seen, is not peculiar to promises; it obtains in other kinds of avoidable harm for which the agent has no defence or excuse. Still the harm done by a breach of promise is in one respect quite different from the harm caused by other wrongs. Whereas in the case of actions consisting of an interference with another's liberty or immunity, the rule broken is one relating to a prohibition formulated with a 'don't', in a breach of promise the harm rather consists of the promisor's not performing an affirmative or positive act, a failure *to do*. The special 'obligatory' element in promise-keeping then seems to enshrine just this positive duty to do rather than not to do. And this, too, may explain why it seems absurd to say that one is under an 'obligation' not to commit murder or trespass, yet not odd at all to say that one is under an obligation to fulfil one's promise, or to do one's job, or to look after one's children and so on. In the latter cases one is referring to something one ought to do, as well as ought to do for particular people (like one's children or one's promisee) —all cases quite unlike those of what one ought not to do, for what one ought not to do one simply abstains from doing; it does not, like a positive obligation, hang or hover over you, constantly reminding you of a duty still remaining to be done.

What we have just said rather confirms the normal assumption that 'I ought to do' and 'I am under an obligation (or under a duty) to do' are logically equivalent, save for the purely linguistic fact that the word 'ought' serves only as a verb, having no noun corresponding to 'obligation' or 'duty'.[16] Even so, are there cases in which 'obligation' does have a special sense, one distinct from because superior to 'ought'? Now one might certainly say that 'I ought to do X, but I have a greater moral obligation not to do it'. But the strength of this does not rest on a special sense of obligation, but on the much simpler difference between legal and moral obligations or oughts (e.g., 'my legal duty as executioner is to shoot X, but morally I ought to let him go'). However there is greater force in another distinction suggested by Warnock. You may say, to give his example, that you 'ought' to give the hitchhiker a lift, while admitting that you are still under no obligation to do so. We speak, according to him, of an obligation where there are clear and inescapable reasons to act as one ought to, where accordingly one feels one is bound so to act, given these reasons, whereas an 'ought' is not quite so decisive or inescapable.[17] If someone says 'You know, you ought to give that hitchhiker a lift', you may still reply: 'Well, I don't share your view. There is no such moral obligation to this effect.' Only where we use 'ought' not in an 'open' but 'settled' sense, that is, settled because now based on an established precedent or practice does the ought turn into an obligation: hence 'you ought to give the hitchhiker a lift' now means 'you are obligated to give him a lift' there being a settled rule that you do. Every 'obligation' thus includes an 'ought', but not every ought an obligation; for some 'oughts' may never become 'obligations': we may endlessly disagree about our 'oughts' to hitchhikers, whereas an 'obligation', as Hume remarked repeatedly, cannot be intelligible unless there already exists an antecedent morality.[18]

LAW AND EQUITY

Moral practices, we have seen, arise from the constant accumulation of moral rules, itself a result of the requirement of universalisability under which moral rules have to be applicable to future cases as we have to treat like cases alike. Universalisability, then, as it accumulates lines of precedent, achieves a profoundly practice-forming or institutionalising effect, quite apart from being a formal condition for reasons and rules to qualify as moral.

Law adds a further stabilising element to moral practices, principally by recording and storing moral decisions as these are made. By recording decisions, law makes these decisions more specific, anchoring them in particular sets of facts, thus sharpening our perceptions of the similarities or differences between cases as well as making the whole process of identifying these similarities and differences both more sophisticated and precise. So in recording decisions law becomes a sort of public repository of moral judgements, a repository which also calls for conceptual systematisation, since the point of the exercise is not to leave the stored decisions in limbo but to publicise connections between old and new grievances, including past and future moral similarities. A 'written' tradition of law is then not only an available record of existing moral rules, not only a constant reminder of what has already been morally judged, it also provides an intellectual or cognitive base from which 'new' decisions and judgements can be made. A 'written' or 'learned' tradition of law thus creates a 'body' of detailed rules, offering knowledge to be consulted, what the Romans called *ratio scripta*; all quite unlike a purely 'oral' tradition which tends to rely on broader 'maxims', or on broader and more easily rememberable 'customs'.

A written tradition has another effect on legal reasoning. Not only does it make law more resistant to change or qualification, it often ushers in a distinction between 'law' and 'equity', equity now assuming a somewhat special role, that of functioning like a procedure charged with continually reforming or rectifying existing legal provisions. Aristotle, as everyone knows, saw equity as a device of restoring justice where justice was not achieved by the law of the law courts.[19] But he was puzzled why such a device should be necessary; his answer, very briefly, was that equity is required to amplify the law because of the generality of the terms in which it has to be formulated; for law, he insisted, can only generalise, since the data of human behaviour are not reducible to uniformity. To some extent this is undoubtedly so. There are situations so special that they call for complete equitable discretion; there are other situations where we ascribe rights or liability on the basis of 'defeasible' concepts that invite a new value-judgement from case to case. As a more general proposition, however, the Aristotelian explanation is not really satisfactory. Though true that legal (or moral) rules must be couched in general terms, in the sense of having to be 'general' enough to satisfy the requirement of universalisability, a rule can still be more or less general or more or less specific, generality or specificity being simply a matter of degree depending on the size of the class of acts to be included.[20] Again, Aristotle's account leaves it unclear how the equity itself is to be expressed. If it is to be more than an *ad hoc* discretion, the equity, too, will have to be couched in general terms, whether it takes the form of a principle or an exception or counter-principle. Indeed, as we have earlier seen, moral and legal rules do not resist qualifications or even exceptions but in fact invite these; rules are not absolute but *prima facie* statements, precisely because, unlike commands, they are supported by reasons regarding the actions they prescribe or proscribe.

Somewhat similar considerations apply to the familiar problem of 'hard cases'. These of course are cases which because of their new or special facts fit ill or hardly into already existing rules, with the consequence that these rules may have to be extended or modified. Thus arose the idea that hard cases make bad law, although in truth, hard cases do not made 'bad' as rather untidy law: untidy in the sense that new exceptions or qualifications disturb the established pattern of written rules. Hard cases, we then discover, do not make 'bad' but 'better' in the sense of 'fuller' law, if only because the exceptions or qualifications which hard cases bring contribute to the equitable rectification of a legal rule. And untidy as such exceptions may at first appear, they too become established, even orthodox, law in their turn. Unfortunately lawyers in over-emphasising the need for legal certainty tend to make of certainty a false ideal, especially where that ideal represents little more than a desire for inertia or an opposition to moral reform as effected by an ongoing equity.[21] Lawyers too easily forget that if law must be certain, it cannot morally stand still: not, obviously, in the sense of having to be constantly overruled, rather in the sense that legal like moral rules always remain subject to refinements or exceptions simply because we cannot avoid reconsidering their scope and implications as new moral problems occur.

6 Moral and Legal Rules

CENSURE AND COERCION

As the practical function of moral no less than of legal rules is
to guide inter-personal conduct according not to purely
personal preferences but to supra-personal principles by
which we want to live, their concomitant objective must be
to discourage or deter morally deviant acts, if only because
normative rules do not operate in a critical vacuum, their
non-compliance rather giving rise to censure or condemnation, sometimes to compulsion or coercion as well. This
objective obviously includes a social determination to make
these rules conformingly effective, in the only way they can
secure even some degree of conformity, namely, by employing external pressure, all of which indeed calls attention to
what we have called their heteronomous element. For, as we
attempted to show in Chapter 1, what distinguishes autonomous from heteronomous rules is that whereas the former
(say, technical or scientific) rules offer criteria for the
achievement of given results which we may or may not wish
to pursue, heteronomous rules are primarily set in a regulative key, as they tell us not how to serve our own interests
but to restrain or modify our personal ends where they
conflict with other ends, in favour of an end shared or
sharable with that of other persons, in particular so socially
crucial an end as that of preventing or at least diminishing
avoidable harm or injury.

Now the censure or condemnation coming in the wake of
heteronomous rules not only express public reactions to
certain events, being in fact vicarious or socialised versions of

the grievances or complaints we voice individually; as critical reactions they also carry with them the moral reason behind the censure, if only because what mobilises the censure, what explains the public reactions, is the social desire to prevent avoidable harm. Of course a moral rule may not be socially effective as it cannot by itself assure compliance, only appropriate human steps or pressures can. In some cases there is sufficient pressure from mere censure or disapproval; in others we need stronger measures of a 'compulsory' or 'coercive' kind. No doubt, we cannot, literally speaking, be 'coerced' into complying with anything; some people can resist any amount of compulsion; hence to speak of censure or coercion is to refer to such punitive acts or threats which, as human experience shows, do have their intended regulative effect since, faced with such threats, we frequently enough do prefer compliance to the pain or shame of a public criticism or penalty. Certainly there are law-abiding citizens who obey moral rules out of conscience or conviction, virtually autonomously. Most of us, however, are less deontologically inclined, often too weak not to be swayed by temptation or self-interest, although still no less capable of understanding that we do a 'wrong' and expose ourselves to blame if our actions cause more or less serious injury.

Indeed both our personal grievances and public reactions closely relate to the magnitude of the harm done. We see this better by distinguishing, very broadly, between (what for present purposes we may call) 'corrigible' and 'incorrigible' causes for complaint. Where A commits some corrigible harm the group may try to correct A's ways by advice or entreaty or persuasion, or (more severely) by a temporary ostracism or boycott, all measures usually adequate enough where we consider the harm or offence, though deserving blame, as an essentially minor one. The offender here deserves no more, but also no less, than a reminder of an existing moral rule; and what we normally call moral censure as distinct from legal sanction seems characteristically concerned with just such corrigible acts. Many of our daily customs, including most of our rules of courtesy or etiquette, deal with acts that possess a ready corrigibility, through an apology perhaps or some other simple act of atonement. The situation greatly alters where the offence is not corrigible, where the action results in a maiming or other serious injury leaving a permanent disability. It is one thing to arrive barefoot at a special dinner, quite another to gouge out another's eye; in the former case your host might be pained by your disrespect for the occasion, in the latter the victim is incorrigibly harmed. Obviously a group or community cannot treat the bully more leniently than the barefoot boor; for if it did we would be unable to understand its moral standards, its scale of harm, as well as what it is at all trying to achieve with its censure or blame.

The greater the harm then the stronger the social reactions; indeed these will be reactions with a distinctive retributive quality. Not that retribution now supersedes deterrence; all social or heteronomous judgements, with their censure and condemnation, inevitably project a deterrent element; retribution now rather represents a particular desire to get even with or punish a particular offender. Needless to say, deterrence and retribution differ in several important respects. By threatening heavier penalties we may hope to deter people, sometimes so effectively that the day of retribution will never come; conversely, we may react retributively, on an angry impulse, without any regard for the deterrent effect of what we do. Deterrence, in other words, is an empirical notion, retribution more strictly a moral response. This apart, however, deterrence and retribution should not be differentiated too rigidly; they can and do go together, especially in serious or incorrigible delicts which we may wish both to be retributive about and to deter. In fact, what deters here is precisely the possibility of retribution as it is just this which invites us to predict the possible (punitive or reactive) effects of our actions and, more particularly, the strength of the criticism or condemnation our actions may produce. It also follows that retribution must be within morally measurable bounds in the sense that there must be some correspondence and proportion between the harm we do and the penalties or sanctions we can incur, if these penalties themselves are to be morally relevant and predictable. Unless this is so, moral rules would not be action-guiding *qua* moral rules; the latter would be nothing more than reports of sundry active and reactive events; moral rules, so-called, would only provide a catalogue of *mala prohibita*; we would not have, nor be able to have, a rational calculus of what constitutes a *malum in se*; our moral rules, to echo Kant, would be like the wooden head in Phaedrus' fable, a head without a brain.[1]

To make the same point in another way, suppose the members of a group were conforming to legal rules purely on deterrent grounds, because (let us say) they empirically or prudentially feared the reactions as painful consequences irrespective of their morality. Even if such a society were possible, what sort of society would it be? We would be living in fear of reactions without knowing why such reactions arise; we might become prudential experts in avoiding unpleasant consequences, acting according to what we could get away with, not according to standards of moral fault or responsibility. It needs little imagination to see what such a way of life would lead to: a state of affairs (one somehow shies away from calling it a human society) in which our rational (but purely selfish or self-regarding) behaviour would make room only for the survival of the fittest, with those perhaps not strong or cunning enough either to survive or at the very least left distinctly disadvantaged: as disadvantaged as the chicken not strong or courageous enough to maintain its place in the pecking-order. We would, in short, be living the kind of life the Greeks attributed to the giants who cultivate justice with the fist.

The fact remains that moral rules do not give rise to heteronomous reactions that are normally more than amorphous or fitful events, so long at any rate as these reactions remain unorganised. Only socially organised reactions acquire an institutional effectiveness or regularity, especially (but this is not a necessary condition) if administered by a special enforcing staff. What is more, moral rules now acquire a sort of games-theoretical probability; as it becomes more certain that crime will not pay, people will behave more predictably both in their own conduct and in their expectations of how others behave.[2] The result is that as critical reactions are superseded by organised coercive sanctions, moral rules turn into social practices usually described as 'law', the word 'law' perhaps trying to catch just this quality of regularity or predictability that law now shares with other (non-legal) laws. Yet even though, as legal positivists constantly point out, coercion is the universal feature of all social orders properly described as legal,[3] it is important not to see legal rules as sharply or basically different from moral ones. Legal rules only go further or beyond moral rules as they employ sanctions to increase their social effectiveness; legal rules are thus not just heteronomous, for moral rules are this too, but are regularly in the sense of being organisedly or sanctionably heteronomous. Nor are legal rules quite alone in this; religious rules, too, often carry a sanction for their breach, not admittedly a social sanction but one relying on divine authority; in fact, the religious sanction is, anthropologically, the forerunner of the legal one: the latter merely secularises the former by replacing an uncertain divine intervention with organised human enforcement both more certain and predictable.

SANCTIONS AND THE LEGAL SYSTEM

Organised sanctions, moreover, affect certain other aspects of legal reasoning. To understand this better, we may distinguish between two types of social structure, what we may call the state- and the group-model. In the latter (typically a stateless or pre-state or 'primitive' society) where special law-enforcement agencies do not normally exist, the group being relatively compact, it can apply its rules collectively or directly. Here a legal rule differs little from moral custom, save for the fact that censure can be extended to coercion. In the other model, that of the state or city, we are dealing with a society of numerical complexity and territorial dispersal, where therefore social power over offending citizens cannot be applied, so to speak, 'immanently' as in the group-model, but has to be applied by specialised officials or agencies. This distribution and delegation of power to officials gives legal rules a new organisational dimension; legal rules have to control the work of officials just as their acts have to be kept functioning according to a systematic order, for without this the state would no longer constitute a single unit. Legal rules, in other words, now become concerned with the 'powers' of officials, their spheres of competence, whether they act as legislators, judges, or policemen, since only these powers tell us whether they act 'validly' or 'invalidly'. The mere fact that some official commands something does not bind the citizen at whom it is addressed unless the command is valid, or has 'legality'. So where an official deprives another of his life by hanging, and we ask why this is a legal act and not murder, the only answer one can give is that the hangman was authorised by a court which in turn was empowered by the criminal law to impose capital punishment, which criminal law is itself promulgated by a legislature which is authorised so to legislate by the constitution, which indeed represents our final authority, the 'basic norm' in Kelsen's language.[4]

To say all this, however, raises a much wider difficulty. Only a little reflection shows that *any* organisational system, not only the state, in fact depends on something like a hierarchical structure, each with its own chain of 'validity'. Suppose a gang of robbers in which the lower rungs only act on orders given by a higher echelon who in turn have their orders handed down from an undisputed leader. It is clear that this structure differs greatly from a state's legal system; but if so, how do we state the difference? Kelsen did say that the basic norm is not 'the product of free invention' but must relate to the 'historically first constitution'. But this only postpones the problem, for the first constitution, too, may give way, quite constitutionally, to a gangster-style dictator who runs the government solely in his own interests, or in those of a small clique or coterie, completely disregarding the interests of the people. Does, then, such a government qualify as one fully valid or legitimate; and if it does, how again does this differ from our gang of robbers who (let us suppose) also have a written constitution, one conceivably even with detailed instructions as to how a chief is to be appointed or succeeded? Merely to ask this question at once shows that an appeal to a 'basic norm', whether in Kelsen's or in some modified version, cannot be our complete explanation, that, more importantly, we have to say something more if we are to distinguish a legal from a gangster-style system. What, in particular, we now can say is that a legal system has to rest on what may perhaps be called a 'politico-moral' constitution, that is, one which, unlike a 'constitution' of a gang of robbers, is created by a people or their representatives as well as designed to serve that people as a whole, their common interest. However misguided such a constitution may other-wise be, it must at the very least show some concern for a common good; it cannot merely serve the self-chosen purposes of a few self-appointed individuals, for if it did the system would not be one of law but one virtually of slavery.

It follows, to put this in broader terms, that legal rules, for all their coerciveness, cannot simply be peremptory com-mands, but must primarily regulate reciprocal human behaviour for the broad moral purpose of discouraging the doing of avoidable harm. And it also follows, to mention this only briefly, that we do not owe obedience to law unless this fulfils, at least to some extent, the moral conditions for which it exists. In particular, a coercive system merely designed to suppress its subjects for the exclusive benefit of a ruling clique can morally have no claim to being obeyed, for the simple reason that the whole point of the obedience or conformity that legal rules try to achieve through coercion is not to obtain obedience for its own sake, nor to establish social 'peace' just for the sake of such a peace; its moral point is rather to underpin a social or heteronomous determination to prevent the infliction of inter-personal injury, this obviously for the actual or putative welfare of the whole community. In the kind of regime now under consideration precisely this social and moral aim is missing conspicuously.

We have said that to enable state officials to administer the law uniformly, as regards both themselves and their rule-subjects, there must be rules that confer upon them appropriate 'powers', including rules that determine whether such powers are issued validly. The question therefore is how these rules, all belonging to a class we usually call constitutional rules, can still be regarded as legal since they are not themselves coercive or sanctionable? Or, to put the same question in John Austin's terms, how is constitutional law 'law properly so called' and not just 'positive morality'?[5] The answer seems less difficult than usually imagined. For one thing, such constitutional rules, as they determine the working of the coercive order, are closely dependent on that order, so that while they are not themselves coercive, they are still the rules organising the coercive system. For another, though as system-organising rules they are not action-guiding in a regulative way, they nevertheless guide action in constitutive ways: they tell us what is 'right' or 'wrong', 'valid' or 'invalid', for officials to do. Of course constitutive rules may change, simply as the forms of power-distribution may change; what does not change is the monopoly of coercion retained by the state, unless a power-struggle disturbs or dissolves this monopoly, in which case we are in a revolutionary situation in which constitutive rules no longer obtain. Short of this, however, it does not really matter how often constitutive rules change, provided the law continues as a coercive system organised around and administered by officials.

STATUTES, JUDGES AND LEGAL LOGIC

Another feature of our state-model is that it makes room for quite different sorts of law. First, there are laws, whether called statutes, decrees, ordinances, orders etc. which, as these denominations imply, are imposed from above, imperatively, as the emanations of a legislature or government holding sovereign power for the time being. Second, there are laws made not so much by governments but by judges, the law now consisting of judicial decisions in response to grievances. As everyone knows, judges are often (even increasingly) called upon to apply or interpret statutes or other legislative instruments; but the historic or classical function of the judge, or (so we shall say at any rate) his principal role, is, in the old-fashioned phrase, to do justice between man and man. This judicial role becomes particularly visible in the absence of statute or even under a statute whose provisions do invite judicial creativity.

Statutory interpretation need not long detain us; on the whole, it throws little light on legal reasoning, as it only shows legal reasoning at its most deductive or formally syllogistic. Where the judge's duty is to construe a statute so as to apply it to certain facts, the statute can be seen as the major premise, and the applicable facts as the minor premise. Interpretation of course presupposes that the statutory text is complete and fully relevant, even if not entirely clear on the face of it, or that the text can be seen as complete if viewed against a background of well-defined legal concepts; conceptual jurisprudence (or *Begriffsjurisprudenz*) has been just such an attempt to make major premises more quickly entailable. The minor premise, too, can be made more certain if enriched by appropriate statutory definitions. If, for example, stealing by night is to be a serious crime, or drunken driving, it will help to make the words 'night' and 'drunken' more factually specific. The obvious corollary is that interpretation stops where the statutory text is plain or obvious: *interpretatio cessat in claris.*[6]

More interesting is the question as to what happens if the statutory words are less easily interpretable. According to an old civilian tradition the deductive process can now be assisted by a number of logical devices in the shape of special arguments, which severally and jointly are sometimes supposed to constitute what is known as 'legal logic'. The three most familiar devices here are the argument *per analogiam*, the argument *e contrario* and the argument *a maiore ad minus*. To give an example of the first two, take a statute ordering young 'men' to enlist in the army; the reference to 'men' might include young women if we employ an argument from analogy which could extend men to women at least for the purposes of this statute; on the other hand, 'men' would exclude women were we to reason *e contrario* which clearly vetoes analogous extensions. This example also shows that these arguments, far from doing the logical job expected of them, namely that of demonstrating *one* necessary inference, leave it completely open which argument is to apply, thus allowing quite contradictory conclusions. Nor is the argument *a maiore ad minus*, often regarded as the principal or strongest device in this context, really more successful. For this, again, makes the inference depend on purely teleological considerations, since before we can tell whether or not a new instance is included in, or envisaged by, the major premise we have first to decide whether that premise is to be taken widely or narrowly.[7] It follows that neither logic nor legal logic is now very helpful just as it is clear that the judge cannot construe a statute unless he looks for its wider purpose or direction, in particular the 'mischief' it seeks to obviate. The judge has of course considerable independence where the statute issues only broad or suggestive principles, what the French aptly call *principes féconds* or *fructueux*, which it is left for the courts to develop as new cases arise. Even here, however, judical interpretation remains a 'positivistic' exercise, for the judge is still only construing a statute, albeit according to its spirit, not its letter. The judge, in other words, is still bound by the legislative intent which he is unable to override.

This brings us back to the judge's role in a case-law system such as that of the common law where a judge has the very special task of actually judging situations by a process of reasoning from and towards precedents. It is true that, in actual practice, statutory interpretation and precedent-reasoning are sometimes not easily distinguishable; a statute may contain gaps or very general or abstract provisions (like the *principes féconds* just mentioned) which the judge has to fill in or concretise; also there are not a few instances where statutes are so overlaid with case-law that it is hard to separate the judge-made parts from the legislative provisions. However this may be, it is theoretically still essential to distinguish the interpretation of a statute from judge-made or case-law, because the latter is not so much positivistic as, rather, naturalistic in character: naturalistic because the process of reasoning is not here one of deduction but one of reasoning purely by way of similarity or difference, that is, by way of precedents and principle and exception, in ways we earlier tried to explain. Nor would it be correct to look upon this kind of judicial reasoning as deduction of perhaps a looser sort, as a sort of deduction from so-called 'open' premises; the reason is that such 'open' deduction does not really amount to anything logically significant, for if the major premise is truly 'open' deduction simply becomes a vacuous exercise. Nor, again, would it be right to say that a judge's *ratio decidendi* represents a working hypothesis that can dovetail with a (Popperian) hypothetico-deductive scheme; for the unanswered question remains how we arrive at a *working* hypothesis from which a new decision is relevantly deducible. In fact, to characterise the judge's role as deductive comes dangerously near to what can only be described as the 'positivistic fallacy' under which a judge would be treating a previous decision as if it were a statute, or establishing his own decision as if it were one. In judicial case-law, we have argued before, the judge follows a process of reasoning very much as would a natural lawyer as he is comparing old and new cases in terms of their similarities or differences which is in fact in terms of their moral attributes.

More importantly still, not to appreciate the differences between statute law and case-law is to overlook crucial differences of the legal and logical features which they possess respectively. Statutory rules depend, as we have seen, on their 'legality' or 'validity', that is, on the power of the authority legislating them. Such rules, accordingly, have to be issued or promulgated; their operation begins at a certain time just as they can expire after their specified duration; one statutory rule can repeal, replace, revise, amend another, while a later rule supersedes an earlier (*lex posterior derogat priori*) if they are in conflict.[8] Above all, since only promulgated rules can claim to exist, it follows that punishable actions must be legislated for, to enable rule-subjects to know in advance what they may or must not do, which of course is the meaning of the well-known maxim: *nulla poena sine lege*. The rules emerging from case-law, on the other hand, are much less concerned with validity or promulgation, for case-law rules do not have, at least not in the same formal sense, a beginning and an end; representing as they do *mala in se* rather than *mala prohibita*, the 'wrongs' they prohibit rest on moral judgements supported by arguments, arguments which can be right or wrong. Indeed case-law rules do not begin or cease to be right or wrong; they are what they are, so to speak, timelessly. They are what they are also irrespective of superior authority; even where a higher court overrules a lower, it does so not *qua* superior legislator but because the lower court was 'wrong', wrong on principle. Thus while *mala prohibita* can themselves be unjust, it would be a contradiction in terms to characterise *mala in se* as immoral; hence case-law rules are not caught by the rule of *nulla poena sine lege*, precisely because *mala in se* do not have to be promulgated beforehand.

To see this better, consider a well-known criminal case. A Mrs Manley falsely told the police she had been robbed, as a result of which several innocent people were brought under suspicion, the police wasting a lot of time investigating the complaint. She was prosecuted and convicted for acts constituting a public mischief.[9] This was a crime which though not completely unknown nevertheless rested on only a few *dicta* in old cases which did not cover the present facts. The decision gave rise to considerable controversy on the ground that it constituted retroactive law-making. One view was that retrospective laws are always unjustified, while on another view such laws are only pernicious if they introduce liability for conduct which might well have been different had the agent known of the subsequent law; so if we do not believe that Mrs Manley would have conducted herself differently had she known what the law either was or might later be, the fact that it was retroactive cannot make any moral difference.[10] However the latter view, too, does not really help as it avoids the real problem simply by advancing the most convenient hypothesis. If, instead, we assume that Mrs Manley would have acted differently had she known what might legally happen, how can we *then* say that the subsequent decision against her was still not 'pernicious' but morally justified?

The answer seems simple enough. Surely Mrs Manley could have been told that though true that there was, when she did what she did, no specific crime expressly covering her conduct, and though also true that judge-made law has been less quick to declare new criminal (as distinct from civil) wrongs, it has never been beyond the wit of judges to condemn conduct which, like Mrs Manley's, was deliberately harmful; she could have guessed that her false accusations would damagingly affect some innocent people as well as waste a lot of policemen's time. So her action, though not covered by a *malum prohibitum*, did nevertheless constitute a *malum in se*. Contrary to what is sometimes maintained, retrospective law-making is then not always a 'necessary evil'; it is necessary, but no evil, for what distinguishes such retrospective decisions is that they do not penalise the unsuspecting but rather remind us of the continuing moral point that we must avoid doing things that may cause harm to others.

We now also see that what gives case-law its often very remarkable qualities of logical consistency and coherence is not its employment of something special or extraneous called legal logic; these logical qualities rather result from case-law's remarkable fidelity to a basic moral theme that systematically connects old with new legal rules and so animates a large and central part of the whole case-law enterprise. There is however also another kind of 'legal logic' which fulfils quite a different function and applies both to statute and to judge-made law. It is a logic not concerned with inference or deduction but rather with system or order, with the analytical ordering of the material. The logical task here is to pool and classify the legal material from all sources, to arrange it according to particular trouble-areas or common subject-matter, for the sake of obtaining a better overall view as well as of making the material more accessible and usable. As our legal material is nowadays assuming quite massive proportions, its ordering or clarification has become a major undertaking. In any case, mass creates its own complexity; legal reasoning must perform a somewhat different role with the emphasis now on logical or conceptual economy, on technical simplicity, or more broadly on the 'elegance' of the law. The legal analyst here approaches his material rather in the way a philosopher of science approaches scientific results, both being concerned with their respective results *ex post facto* rather than *in fieri*. Of course conceptual analysis can be well or ill performed, or can be more or less useful or illuminating. But this is another story.

BORDERLINE CASES AND MORAL NEUTRALITY

There remain some very important situations where a judge, or a person trying to act like a judge, cannot decide a case on the basis of its moral features, but will have to decide in a morally neutral manner. In the first place, a judge may have to reach a decision on mainly prudential considerations, a good example being the evidentiary questions relating to the minor premise, i.e. questions as to whether an alleged delict has in fact been committed, including such difficulties as the admissibility of certain evidence, or its probative value, or the credibility or corroboration of witnesses. Obviously these are difficulties which seek an empirically feasible or wise solution, and which do not therefore raise a specifically moral problem, unless the further question arises (but a question we need not now pursue) whether the burden of proof is 'fairly' distributed, whether one side (defender or accuser) is not being disadvantaged. In the second place, however, a judge may be driven into, or adopt a stance of, moral neutrality even with regard to a basic principle or major premise because he is unable or unprepared to reach a moral decision on the given facts. This characteristically happens in what we may describe as 'borderline cases', of which we shall mention two instances in particular: one where a case defies a clear *pro* or *con* decision, situated as it is in what is still a penumbral intermediate area; the other where a judge has to deal with a principle that offers no moral calculus for determining its limits or scope.

Borderline cases pose, especially for law, a most important problem. On the one hand, it is clear that the judge does have to decide as he cannot, unlike an academic moralist, cultivate his tortured uncertainty to the point of refusing a decision; such a refusal would in effect amount to the rejection of a claim or grievance without this rejection even being justified. On the other hand, the borderline case denies him the moral reasons he needs to support his decision for or against a claimant; nor can the judge now appeal to prudential grounds for these are strictly irrelevant. But since a judge has to give some reason for whatever he decides, what can these reasons be? The only alternative is for him to resort to reasons of a 'conceptual' or 'categorial' kind, that is, reasons of physical or factual, yet excluding all moral (or prudential) content. The judge, that is to say, will now deal with the case solely on its physical or spatio-temporal characteristics, classifying these according to ordinary 'psychological' or 'commonsense' criteria, namely, whether the new case resembles another (earlier) case in the way two objects or events resemble each other in space and time.[11] In fact, the law books carry many instances of such reasoning: to give only one example we have given before, that of vicarious liability. Where a servant injures another, his master becomes additionally (vicariously) liable unless (and this is now the operative exception) the servant can be said to have acted 'on a frolic of his own', outside the 'course of employment'. What, then, is such a frolic? As it is immaterial whether the servant acted 'for' the master, or in 'his' interest or for 'his' (rather than the servant's own) purposes, it follows that a 'frolic' can only be defined in a sort of lexical way, comparatively to other instances described as 'frolics' in circumstances more or less similar. Thus a major detour may be regarded as a frolic, unlike a minor one, the difference between major and minor chiefly resting on such factual considerations as whether the detour was (spatially or temporally) extensive or whether it was relatively more limited.

In these circumstances, it will be clear, such concepts as 'course of employment' and 'frolic' take on a very technical character, inevitably so since the categories in question here develop in a lifeless, almost arid, context precisely because the relevant similarities or differences between situations now rest on facts to which no moral or social point is attributable. Rife as technical conceptualism thus becomes, it is nevertheless an unavoidable phenomenon, also a phenomenon, though eminently characteristic of law, not entirely confined to it; for a similar conceptualist process is bound to occur in any normative system in which a judge or similar official cannot decide a case, though decide he must, not having any moral (or, for that matter, even prudential) grounds on which to support a decision. In law itself, a great deal of what is often seen as being particularly 'technical' or 'pure' law derives from a morally neutral conceptualism on or around the borderlines. It may even be the case that, as a matter solely of bulk or quantity, morally neutral or borderline concepts and cases play a very significant part in the law, no less a part than morally inspired rules. Still, it is vital to remember that legal rules would make, overall, little or no sense if seen as morally 'pure', as if law could flourish in a moral vacuum. The main thrust in legal reasoning, above all in case-law reasoning, cannot go forward without a moral direction or theme; indeed we could not even have borderline cases unless we were already committed to firm *pro* and *con* positions on certain issues or acts; what we here do not have, at least not yet, is any clear idea of where exactly the borderline between these opposing moral positions is to be, or how wide it is to be.

THE PRIMACY OF RIGHTS

We will now have seen that a legal rule performs a dual role, primarily a moral as well as a coercive or sanctionable one: a twofold role which indeed closely corresponds to the distinction between being (morally) under an obligation, or obligated, and being (coercively) obliged. To say that a person is obligated is to say that he ought not to do this or that, whether or not he is actually, or coercively, obliged to do what he ought, while to ask whether a person is in fact obliged is to ask an empirical question, to what extent he is effectively obliged, or is (prudentially or otherwise) prepared to run the risk of a sanction, of having the law enforced against him. But even if he manages to avoid the latter risk, this does not affect the 'existence' of a legal rule in the first sense of 'ought'; even if a person is not obliged in an empirical or prudential sense, he is nevertheless still under the other 'ought' which, if it is to be 'obligatory' at all, cannot now but be a moral ought. Without this dual sense of the legal ought, we could never say that a person commits an illegal act even where law enforcement may have practically broken down.

Yet another aspect of this duality is this: that while a person can be (coercively) obliged to do what a rule requires him to do, he cannot be (morally) obligated to do or not to do something unless somebody else has a right to it, that somebody being usually another person, in some cases the group or society as a whole (as mainly in criminal law). For example, I may be coercively ordered and thus obliged to dig holes in quicksand, but I may be under no moral obligation so to do: nobody would blame me if I stopped pursuing this senseless activity. Thus to understand the moral aspect of legal rules is also a key to understanding what we shall describe as the primacy of rights, meaning not only that rights come first in the moral and legal scale of things, but also that duties are not explicable by themselves, that (in other words) they are, typically and overwhelmingly, only responses to rights, except of course such purely coercive duties (as that in our quicksand example) which however are duties for which one can give no other justifying reason than that of brute force. In this light, it then seems no accident that, in many European languages, the word for 'law' is 'right' or 'rights' — *jus, Recht, droit, diritto, derecho*. In this light, again, it cannot be true, at any rate not in the full sense of what Bentham meant by saying that: 'whatever business the law may be conversant about, may be reduced to one sort of operation, viz. that of creating duties'.[12] On the contrary, it is rights that have first to be identified before duties can be said to exist, because both in law and morals we are primarily concerned with human wants and grievances; it is they which create our disputes including the need to decide or settle them.

If not explicitly, the primacy of rights is perhaps more often recognised implicitly: recognised implicitly, it appears, in what is known as the 'benefit-theory' of rights, the theory, very broadly, that with the exception of such doubtful duties as the duty not to commit suicide all other duties are meant to benefit the correlative holders of rights. It is true that this

theory has been severely criticised, mainly on the ground that
if a right-holder is no more than the intended beneficiary of a
duty, this clearly makes 'right' an unnecessary term in
the law, since the indispensable terminology of 'duty' would
say better all that can and need be said.[13] For, so the same
criticism continues, no purpose is served in translating a duty
(say) not to murder or steal into the corresponding right not
to be murdered or stolen from: does not the mere awkward-
ness of these right-statements show the greater aptitude of
duty-talk? Still linguistic usage or convenience is not always
the best guide to logical truth. Here, surely, the important
point is that there would be no duties unless there are not just
corresponding but in fact prior rights. Thus such terms as
'murder', 'theft' or 'trespass' specify an injury to the right-
holder; the whole initiative for redress comes, as it always
has, from him. In many cases, needless to say, we do not speak
of a victim's rights; instead of saying that the murdered man
has a right not to be killed, we rather say that the murderer
violated the duty not to kill. However the explanation of this
is not that rights are here redundant, but that the injury has
come to be fully expressible in the duty alone. In other cases,
we cannot even speak of a duty to do or refrain, since we
cannot identify the particular action to be done or forborne,
although we can still speak of a right not to be harmed.
Where, as we have seen, a master is held liable for an injury to
another caused by his servant in the course of employment,
we do not say that the master should not have employed that
servant, or that the master was negligent, for he may have
been careful; we merely say that the master is liable for the
damage provided certain conditions are fulfilled. Not only
here, but in most cases of 'strict' or 'absolute' liability it is
often impossible to pinpoint the exact duty or action on
which a defendant's responsibility could be said to rest.[14]

The primacy of rights also puts in perspective other
activities we naturally pursue to satisfy our wants. Daily
activities such as walking, eating, dreaming, are not normally
called rights; here we do what we can, without there being

any 'must' or 'may' about it. Only where the exercise of these activities is hindered or threatened do we resort to the terminology of a right, precisely to affirm that we *may* walk, talk, eat, etc., since it becomes again important to stress that we 'may' do these things, not merely that we 'can' do them. Simple as all this is, much of it has become somewhat obscured in recent legal philosophy where a sharp distinction is drawn between a 'liberty' and a 'right', the former (putting this very briefly) taken to be the denial or limitation of a duty, the latter simply the correlative of one. On this view it can never make any sense to speak of a 'right' to eat or sleep etc. since such a right does not include a claim against another (like a claim to a sum of money one is owed); eating, sleeping, walking etc. are accordingly more accurately described as 'permissions' or 'liberties'. Thus one has a liberty to walk or talk just as one is at liberty or permitted to wear a dog-collar or medals so long as there is no law against it: one is not committing a delict in now doing what one does. Though true as far as it goes, this distinction between a liberty and a right, from the exclusive point of view of how either relates to duty, greatly exaggerates the difference between them. A liberty, to explain this a little further, is not just the limitation of a duty even though, uninterestingly, it is that too. To refer to a liberty is, more significantly, to deny a duty in a much fuller sense. For example, to deny that a father is under a duty to chastise his child is not to say that he is under a duty not to chastise it, but that he has no duty at all in this respect: he may chastise it or not. In this sense the father's 'liberty' to chastise, precisely because of this element of choice, rather duplicates what would be asserted by a corresponding 'right'. Furthermore, to refer to such a liberty is also to assert that it is protected, at least to some extent, in which sense, again, the liberty constitutes something very similar to a right. My liberty to walk or talk is protected not, it is true, by an exactly correlative duty, but is protected by a more general duty, imposed on everyone, not to interfere with another person's normal peaceable activities.

The position is similar in the following example often cited in support of the alleged difference. Suppose two persons (you and I) are running to pick up a gold watch, each trying to pick it up first. Since here, it is said, neither party can claim a right to take the watch first, either has only a liberty to do so; hence if you pick it up first, you only interfere with my liberty but not with my right to do the picking up; hence you commit no delict against me in picking it up first.[15] However, this example does not show what it intends to show. To speak here of a liberty means not only that I can or may run to pick up the gold watch first, it means, more specifically, that nobody can stop me, not even you, my competitor. Thus the real point of the liberty is to protect my *opportunity* to pick up the watch first, an opportunity which I may, or may not, be able to seize successfully. But in any case while I am about this opportunity my liberty serves as a warning to you not to trip me up, though you may be sorely tempted to do so on the wrong understanding that because I admittedly have no right *to* the watch before having picked it up, I have therefore also no protected right in the sense of an opportunity to pick it up. And similarly the right to compete, too, it has been suggested, has led to false reasoning since even great judges have been misled to say that a person is 'entitled' to carry on trade 'freely', and so, making use of the ambiguity of 'entitled', have fallaciously converted a mere 'liberty' into a 'right'.[16] But where is the alleged fallacy? Surely the trader has not just a liberty to trade freely, he does have a right not to be interfered with in this liberty. In any case it seems pointless to speak of the trader here having a mere liberty, as we are not even concerned to say that he is under no duty (has a 'no-duty') not to compete. Had he been under a duty not to compete, the lifting of that duty would have been worth stating, but this is not what the present problem is about. What it is about is whether one trader may trade freely if this interferes with another trader also trying to trade freely on his side. In other words, the question now is precisely one about a right since it is about whether, or to

what extent, one can trade 'freely' without unduly interfering with another's corresponding rights.

MORAL AND LEGAL THEORY

We have given legal theory a large moral task, and to moral
theory perhaps a new perception of how closely connected it
is with law. When lawyers argue about what they call 'the
merits' of a case, or when judges decide a case, that is, judge a
case in a strict sense of judging rather than merely apply or
interpret a statute, they engage in a form of reasoning which
is admittedly legal but which also coincides with moral
reasoning. For their business now being with *mala in se*, not
with *mala prohibita*, they are inevitably bound to argue like
moral naturalists or natural lawyers. Thus, contrary to what
legal positivists often assert, morality is not just another so-
called 'source' of law, a source like statute or custom; over a
large and central area law is in fact applied morality.

Nor does this require us to reject positivism, only to
recognise that positivism and naturalism are not mutually
exclusive and that, more significantly still, we very much
need both doctrines for an adequate explanation of legal
rules. Without positivism, and its principal assertion that laws
are valid simply by coming down from a higher (political)
authority, we could not even describe certain laws, statutes in
particular, as unjust or immoral; indeed on a strictly
naturalistic basis to speak of unjust or immoral laws is
virtually self-contradictory, if only because unjust laws
cannot 'naturally', they can only 'positivistically' exist. Again
we need some form of positivism, with its emphasis on
political organisation and officials, to explain the coercive
dimension so characteristic of one, though only one, of two
aspects of law; even power-conferring rules, though not
coercive themselves, presuppose, just as they are parasitic on,
the existence of coercive rules. If, however, we next ask how
judges make their law, that is, case-law wholly distinct from

statute law, the answer cannot be that they always act like legislators exercising a law-making discretion, for this would simply vacate their role as judges. Indeed only a naturalist theory allows us to say that judges may act purely as judges, that is, judges making decisions according to reasons which can be supported or justified on their own grounds precisely because they are moral reasons.

Just as naturalism retrieves for law an integral moral element, so law rescues for morality an important naturalist perspective. For attention to law refocuses our view of human affairs upon our perennial trouble-cases, including the rules and arguments we use and only can use for the settling of disputes and grievances, above all grievances about actions of avoidable harm. It is true that this is not the whole of morality. There are other moral areas such as have to do with ideals of human society, or with the virtues we aspire to whenever we blame ourselves for perhaps lacking in forti-tude, or moderation, or generosity. Still, shortcomings as to the kind of persons we want *to be* are very different from grievances about the harmful things we can *do*: the latter, surely, are socially our basic grievances, those with which morality, whatever else it does, must primarily come to terms.

Notes

CHAPTER 1

1. Of course if a rule or reason is intelligible, it will also be informative, but the converse is not true: S. Körner, *Categorical Frameworks* (Oxford: Blackwell, 1970) p. 63.
2. Hume, *Enquiries Concerning the Human Understanding*, 2nd ed., Selby-Bigge (ed.) App. I, v (Oxford: 1902).
3. This is sometimes called an 'anankastic' proposition. See G. H. von Wright, *Norm and Action* (London: 1963) p. 10, where technical are further distinguished from hypothetical rules, e.g. 'If the dog barks, don't run', a sentence normally used for prescribing a certain mode of conduct should a certain contingency happen. Whether von Wright helpfully classifies the various kinds of rules in the way he does is another question; he does seem to lack a general framework or theory to justify his particular classification, a criticism already made by Alf Ross, *Directives and Norms* (London: 1968) p. 78.
4. T. Beardsworth, "'Ought' and Rules" (1970) 45, *Philosophy*, pp. 240–1.
5. For 'appetitive' questions, see A. Quinton, *The Nature of Things* (London: 1973) p. 360.
6. *Nichomachean Ethics*, book 5, ch. 7.
7. J. R. Searle, *Speech Acts* (Cambridge: 1969) pp. 50–52.
8. Ibid., pp. 33–5.
9. 'The rules for checkmate in chess . . . must define *checkmate in chess* in the same way that the rules of . . . chess define 'chess' – which does not, of course, mean that a slight change in a fringe rule makes it a different game; there will be degrees of centrality in any system of constitutive rules' (Ibid., p. 34).
10. In Kant's *Grundlegung*, of course, the two words are used to describe our two kinds of will: our autonomous will being the same as our practical reason, the 'heteronomy of the will' rather referring to our desires or inclinations etc.; see Kant, *The Moral Law* (London: Paton transl., 1947) pp. 70, 88 *passim*.
11. See J. R. Cameron, "'Ought' and Institutional Obligation" (1971) 46, *Philosophy*, p. 309.

12. Searle, op. cit., pp. 33 – 5 who also maintains that constitutive rules make possible *new* forms of behaviour (such as, in particular, new games), but that regulative rules are more concerned with *existing* conduct (the rules against criminal or deviant behaviour being the simplest instances here). However even new rules of games do not so much create new forms of behaviour as, rather, new kinds of games; while regulative rules, too, may be concerned to change things for the future; in fact, many of our social rules do just this; of the latter one can indeed say what Kierkegaard said of life, that it 'must be lived forwards but can only be understood backwards'. For similar criticisms of Searle, see Christopher Cherry, 'Regulative Rules and Constitutive Rules' (1973) 23, *Phil. Quart.*, pp. 301, 309; G. J. Warnock, *The Object of Morality* (London: 1971) pp. 37– 38.

13. See H. L. A. Hart, *The Concept of Law* (Oxford: 1961) p. 24; A. Quinton, *The Nature of Things* (London: 1973) p. 364.

14. See more fully H. N. Castañeda, 'Ought and Moral Oughts' (1965) 41, *A.R.S.P.* pp. 201, 204.

CHAPTER 2

1. See H. Sidgwick, *The Methods of Ethics*, 7th ed. (London: 1972) p. 25ff.

2. M. G. Singer, *Generalisation in Ethics* (London: 1963) p. 303.

3. Hume, *A Treatise of Human Nature*, Selby-Bigge (ed.) II, iii, 3 (Oxford: 1888).

4. Kant, *The Moral Law* (Paton transl.) p. 56.

5. See Leslie Stephen, *The Science of Ethics* (London: 1882) pp. 206– 7.

6. For this Dilemma, see R. D. Luce and H. Raiffa, *Games and Decisions* (New York: 1958) ch. 5; for the moral aspects, A. K. Sen, 'Choice, Ordering and Morality' in S. Körner (ed.), *Practical Reason* (Oxford: Blackwell, 1974) p. 54ff.

7. J. J. C. Smart and B. Williams, *Utilitarianism For and Against* (Cambridge: 1973) p. 30ff.

8. Ibid., pp. 39– 42.

9. Hume, *A Treatise of Human Nature*, III, i, 1.

10. R. M. Hare, *Freedom and Reason* (Oxford: 1963) pp. 90– 5.

11. *Op. cit.*, p. 105.

12. According to another, slightly different, version of the golden rule argument, what one has to consider is what I would have others do in their treatment of me 'in abstraction from any of my particular desires', so that I apply the 'same principle or standard' to them 'as I would have them apply in their treatment of me' (M. G. Singer, *The Golden Rule* (1963) 38, *Philosophy* pp. 293, 300). On this basis, it is

argued, the rule does not authorise an eccentric or quarrelsome person who loves to be provoked to go about provoking others; on the contrary, he must take account and respect the wishes of people who do not like to be provoked; or, more briefly, he must not annoy others just as he would not like to be annoyed. But this does not really advance matters. As Singer admits, it may not be easy to get a quarrelsome person to see this, if only because he may like to inflict and to suffer certain forms of annoyance on others, yet object to certain forms of annoyance which do not annoy others but are peculiar to him.

13. Hare, op. cit., p. 111.

14. See also G. J. Warnock, *Contemporary Moral Philosophy* (London: 1967) pp. 45–6.

15. The above criticism should not obscure two insights of Hare's: one, his point about imagination which we shall meet again, though in different form, when we come to speak of normativity (in Chapter 3); the other, his insistence on universalisability as a condition of moral reasoning, though this too we shall later explain somewhat differently, as a formal condition of moral rules.

16. Kant, *The Moral Law* (Paton trans.) p. 68n. Under the golden rule, in Kant's view, a criminal would be able to dispute a judge's right to send him to prison. But this does not really hold; for the judge can here easily reply that he, too, would have to go to prison had he done what the criminal did.

17. Kant, op. cit., pp. 43, 50, 52, 57, 88–9, 93–4; and see also his earlier *Lectures on Ethics* (London: 1930) p. 37.

18. Kant, op. cit., pp. 54–5.

19. See Singer, op. cit., pp. 232–3. Professor Singer has, however, argued that this inconsistency need not necessarily result from the categorical imperative itself, on broadly three scores. (i) Kant seems to have been misled by his own unhappy choice of language: 'From "categorical" as opposed to "hypothetical" it is a short step to "unconditional" as opposed to "conditional"', (op. cit., pp. 223–4). (ii) All that Kant really can show is that it is *generally* wrong to lie, not that it is *always* wrong; that it is always wrong cannot in fact be shown (ibid., p. 231). (iii) Because Kant's argument is question-begging, for he is now universalising in order to obtain substantive moral principles, but these depend on 'wrong' or 'injury' to others; yet 'whether it would be wrong is precisely the point in question' (ibid., p. 229). Without getting too involved in textual interpretations, one may point out: As to (i), that Kant did regard his universal law as a 'law *of nature*' which, in this context, could not allow of exceptions, for only unconditional laws are laws of nature.

As to (ii), that if Kant can only show that it is 'generally' wrong to lie, this not only destroys his conception of a 'law' as in (i), but also requires further criteria when it is, and when it is not, wrong to lie which criteria his categorical imperative is not even supposed to furnish. As to (iii), that Singer's point, though well taken, is of much wider application as it extends not only to Kant's argument as above but even to Singer's own generalisation argument, just as it does to universalisability itself seen as a purely formal requirement. We deal with this in detail in Chapter 3.

20. Singer, op. cit., pp. 279–80.
21. Ibid.
22. *Lectures on Ethics*, p. 42.
23. Hare, op. cit., p. 84; and see ibid., pp. 72, 76–7, 79, 82.

CHAPTER 3

1. The position is not the same where the grievances we advance, or the rights we assert, are not directed against harm-causing agents but arise from certain states of affairs. But this raises different questions, more closely connected with distribution, with which we deal in Chapter 5.
2. Hare, *Freedom and Reason*, pp. 10–12.
3. Ibid., p. 107.
4. See C. D. Broad, *Five Types of Ethical Theory* (London: 1930) p. 223; F. H. Bradley, *Collected Essays* (Oxford: 1935) i, p. 100.
5. Singer, op. cit., p. 18–23.
6. Nor is Singer more helpful in his assertion that generality is not a special characteristic of moral judgements but applies to other judgements as well, and that just as a statement 'the plane crashed because its wings fell off' presupposes the generalisation 'whenever a plane's wings fall off it will crash', so moral judgements are analogous to causal judgements as they too have 'this characteristic of implicit generality': see ibid., at pp. 37–8, 51ff. But, surely, these two sorts of generality are quite dissimilar. In scientific judgements we may have better or worse reasons for what we objectively accept to be the case, this always depending on the evidence and the knowledge we have. How does this compare with moral judgements: in what sense are moral reasons similarly true or untrue? Singer gives us no verification procedure, no criteria of how facts are describable as morally relevant. At a later stage, he certainly insists that the actions or consequences about which we generalise must all be regarded as 'undesirable': ibid., p. 41ff. But is not what is to be

regarded as so undesirable precisely what we have to discuss?

7. 'It is the fact that expectations operate on *both* sides of the relation between a given actor and the object of his orientation which distinguishes social interaction from orientation to non-social objects. This fundamental phenomenon may be called the *complementarity of expectations*, not in the sense that the expectations of the two actors with regard to each other's action are identical, but in the sense that the action of each is oriented to the expectations of the other': T. Parsons and E. Shils (eds.) *Toward a General Theory of Action* (Cambridge, Mass.: 1951) p. 15. It is worth noting that all this is very close to the notion of role-taking (of taking the role of another) in social relationships which has been very prominent in recent sociological theory: see R. H. Turner, *Role-Taking: Process versus Conformity*, in A. M. Rose (ed.), *Human Behaviour and Social Process* (Boston: 1962) pp. 20, 25. Turner particularly wants to show that the concept of role does add moral elements to the conception of social interaction.

8. L. Wittgenstein, *Philosophical Investigations* (Oxford: Blackwell, 1953) p. 88.

9. Kant, *The Metaphysical Elements of Justice* (Ladd trans., 1965) pp. 34–5. H. L. A. Hart, 'Are There Any Natural Rights?' (1955) 64, *Philosophical Rev*. p. 175, defends a similar thesis: that if there are any moral rights at all, there is at least one natural right, the equal right of all men to be free; to have a moral right is thus to be able to limit the freedom of another.

10. See P. F. Strawson, *Freedom and Resentment* (London: 1974) pp. 1, 14.

11. Hume, *Enquiries* IX, I, p. 92; Hare, *Freedom and Reason*, p. 95 and *passim*.

12. This process of aggregation may come about by a sort of social osmosis; something like this in fact appears to have been Hume's view:

We may begin with considering anew the nature and force of *sympathy*. The minds of all men are similar in their feelings and operations, nor can any one be actuated by any affection, of which all others are not, in some degree, susceptible. As in strings equally wound up, the motion of one communicates itself to the rest; so all the affections readily pass from one person to another, and beget correspondent movements in every human creature (*Treatise*, book III, iii, p. 1)

13. *Year Book* 13 Hen. VII, Hilary, fo. 14, pl. 5 (1498).

14. D. Lyons, *Forms and Limits of Utilitarianism* (Oxford: 1965) p. 72ff.

15. Once the harmful purpose is spent, there can however be room for post-condemnatory considerations of an 'extenuating' or 'merciful' kind. We may show mercy because once the harm is done, and the censure or condemnation has taken its course, we may still have some sympathy for the agent as a person: allow him his last cigarette, treat him with special benevolence after he has served his punishment, or give him another chance as in showing mercy to a bankrupt by allowing his re-entry into business to enable him to earn a living again.

16. Bentham, *An Introduction to the Principles of Morals and Legislation* in *A Fragment on Government* (W. Harrison (ed.), Oxford: 1948) pp. 125–7, 129–30, 148, 413. The interrelation of 'harm' and 'pain' requires a brief word of caution. While every harm amounts to pain, not every pain is harm in the sense of an injury to another. People may be deeply pained, without being harmed, where they are distressed by other people's self-regarding conduct, e.g. the desecration of the Sabbath. The libertarian would oppose interference with such self-regarding action because merely of its being disliked; the utilitarian would have to support the majority, however intolerant, if the balance of pain and pleasure is in the latter's favour. Nor can one argue that the utilitarian can overlook such dislikes where the pain is caused by a belief rather than the belief by the pain, for this greatly undervalues already held beliefs together with the fact that much of what we call 'offensive' conduct often depends on existing convictions. It follows that, on utilitarian grounds, even a self-regarding action can be wrong if it causes disproportionate distress to other people. See more fully C. L. Ten, *Self-Regarding Conduct and Utilitarianism* (1977) 55, *Australian Journal of Philosophy*, p. 105.

17. A. Quinton, *Utilitarian Ethics* (London: 1973) p. 74.

18. Hobbes, *Leviathan*, C. B. Macpherson (ed.), ch. 17 (Harmondsworth: 1968).

CHAPTER 4

1. Bentham, *Introduction to the Principles of Morals and Legislation*, pp. 422–3.

2. See G. Vlastos, 'Human Worth, Merit and Equality', in J. Feinberg (ed.), *Moral Concepts* (Oxford: 1969) p. 141.

3. Aristotle, *Politics*, 1280a–1281b; and see Bernard Williams, 'The Idea of Equality', in Feinberg, op. cit., pp. 153, 162.

4. See Mill's *Utilitarianism*, ch. 5.

it somehow without language'; in short, a prior agreement quite unlike any ordinary one in that it does not require the use of language (ibid., pp. 178–9). Yet if the presupposition of an ordinary agreement seems absurd, a silent agreement seems doubly absurd; one cannot silently agree to something unless both sides in fact know what that agreement might be about. Prichard would have been on stronger ground had he merely spoken of a silent agreement or social norm against the infliction of harm (as we did in Chapter 3). But this is quite different from saying (as Prichard in effect does) that we have silently agreed that promises have to be kept.

15. G. J. Warnock, *The Object of Morality* (London: 1971) pp. 106–10.
16. See H. Beran, 'Ought, Obligation and Duty' (1972) 50, *Australian Journal of Philosophy*, p. 207.
17. G. J. Warnock, *The Object of Morality*, p. 94.
18. *A Treatise of Human Nature*, pp. 462n., 467–8, 490–1.
19. *Nichomachean Ethics*, book 5, ch. 10.
20. R. M. Hare, 'Principles' (1972) *Proc. Arist. Soc.* 1, 3ff.
21. See J. R. Lucas, 'Justice', (1972) 47, *Philosophy*, pp. 229, 240–1.

CHAPTER 6

1. Kant, *The Metaphysical Elements of Justice* (Ladd trans., 1965) p. 34.
2. See J. R. Lucas, op. cit., p. 240.
3. H. Kelsen, *General Theory of Law and State* (Cambridge, Mass.: 1949) pp. 15, 25, 50–3.
4. H. Kelsen, *Pure Theory of Law* (Berkeley, Calif.: 1967) pp. 193–4, 199–201, 217–18.
5. J. Austin, *The Province of Jurisprudence Determined*, Hart ed., (London: 1954) p. 123ff.
6. See generally Ch. Perelman, *Logique Judiciaire* (Paris: 1976) p. 36ff.
7. See more fully U. Klug, *Juristische Logic* (Berlin-Göttingen: 1958) p. 137ff; E. Schneider, *Logik für Juristen* (Berlin-Frankfurt: 1965) pp. 167, 181.
8. See O. Weinberger (ed.), H. Kelsen, *Essays in Legal and Moral Philosophy* (Dordrecht, Holland: 1973) p. 228ff.
9. *R. v. Manley* [1933] 1 K.B. 529.
10. R. Cross, *Precedent in English Law*, p. 24ff.
11. See S. Körner, *Categorical Frameworks* (Oxford, Blackwell: 1970) p. 3 and *passim*.
12. Bentham, *Of Laws in General*, H. L. A. Hart (ed.), (London: 1970) p. 249.
13. H. L. A. Hart, 'Bentham on Legal Rights' in *Oxford Essays in*

5. A. Quinton, *Utilitarian Ethics* (London: 1973) p. 76.
6. Though very different in analysis, the conclusions here reached are in some respects, though only in some, similar to the second of Rawls's well-known principles (see *A Theory of Justice* (Oxford: 1972) pp. 60ff, 302ff). The first branch of this second principle requires, very briefly, economic inequalities to be so arranged that they still work out for the greatest benefit of the least advantaged. This does not mean that the advantages must all go up or down by the same amount; rather that the worst-off do not become still worse off as a result of the distribution. Thus, though Rawls does not resort to a notion of needs, the needs of the worst-off, obviously here including the urgent needs of the sick and incapacitated, are catered for. Nor does Rawls use the notion of desert, in fact rejecting it, notwithstanding the fact that the second branch of his second principle specifically requires fair equality of opportunity. It is not really clear how equality of opportunity can function without desert; to give equal opportunities assumes that these will not always be used or seized equally, so that those making better use of them will be entitled to keep the prizes if only because they now 'deserve' them having more effectively seized their opportunities. Rawls's exclusion of 'need' and 'desert' seems also to obscure the exact interrelation between the two branches of his second principle. Since we are to start with the second branch, i.e. with equal opportunities, who are the worst-off who are to benefit under the first branch? And if the worst-off or least advantaged are only to be better rather than worse off, what benefits can they claim if they have not availed themselves of the equal opportunities offered? Rawls rejected 'need' and 'desert', on the one hand, because of his 'original position' theory under which people accept the above principle with its two branches provided they are similarly situated and discuss distribution behind a 'veil of ignorance', without knowledge of the benefits or burdens that may come their way; on the other hand, because he gave 'desert' a distinctly deterministic connotation; to him, the effort a person is willing to make mainly depends on his natural abilities and the limited alternatives thus open to him (see ibid., pp. 311–2).
7. For a similar point, see D. Lyons, *Forms and Limits of Utilitarianism*, (Oxford: 1965) pp. 129, 163.
8. See on this J. W. Chapman, 'Justice and Fairness', in Friedrich and Chapman (eds), *Nomos VI: Justice* (New York: 1963) pp. 147, 155, 158, for an illuminating distinction between fair play or fair procedure and just verdict or just outcome, e.g. a trial is fair but the verdict is unjust.
9. See C. D. Broad, 'On the Function of False Hypotheses in Ethics', 26 *Ethics* (1916) pp. 377–88; and see Lyons, op. cit., p. 172.

10. See on this N. Rescher, *Distributive Justice*, (New York: 1966) p. 90ff.
11. *Miller* v. *Jackson* [1977] 3 W.L.R. 20.
12. *R.* v. *Dudley & Stephens* (1884) 14 Q.B.D. 273.
13. Both examples are suggested by Professor Bernard Williams: see J. J. C. Smart and B. Williams, *Utilitarianism For and Against* (Cambridge: 1973) p. 77.
14. J. J. C. Smart and B. Williams, op. cit., pp. 100–4.
15. See D. D. Raphael, 'The Standard of Morals', (1974) *Proc. Aristotelian Society*, I, 10–11.
16. We return to some of these matters in our discussion of promise-keeping in Chapter 5.

CHAPTER 5

1. Bracton, *De Legibus et Consuetudinibus Angliae*, fo. 1b. If pressed, Bracton might perhaps have said that a case should be a source of law in a way that custom is. Not in the sense that a case should be 'popularly' accepted (for, unlike a custom, it 'emanates' not from the people but from a judge); but in the sense that the rule enshrined in a case is to be as 'regular', and thus as predictable or as referrable to, as a customary rule was then supposed to be.
2. All this has not remained unperceived by at least some lawyers. Thus Goodhart partly, though perhaps only partly, saw this point in his famous essay on determining the *ratio decidendi* where he suggested that facts of person, time, place, etc. are immaterial properties ((1931) 40 Yale Law J. 161). Unfortunately Goodhart also added that such spatio-temporal facts are only normally immaterial, that is, unless the judge states the contrary. But a judge, too, is limited in his determination of material facts. To think differently is due to what we may call the 'positivistic fallacy' which is to think that because judges are often said to 'legislate' that therefore the whole decision is theirs, when in fact it is only *partly* theirs, as they too cannot depart from general standards or rules.
3. For a different view of the relationship between legal precedents and moral rules, see however D. H. Hodgson, *The Consequences of Utilitarianism* (Oxford: 1967) p. 142ff.
4. *Donoghue* v. *Stevenson* [1932] A.C. 562.
5. R. Cross, *Precedent in English Law* (Oxford: 1961) p. 207; E. H. Levi, *Introduction to Legal Reasoning* (Chicago: 1949) p. 2ff.
6. This discussion is much indebted to J. Kovesi: *Moral Notions* (London: 1967) ch. 1, which in this connection revives the

Aristotelian distinction between formal and material elements
7. Kovesi's formal-material distinction does not really succee eliminating the descriptive-evaluative distinction as it is appar intended to do. It is one thing to say that evaluative elements ser formal elements of moral notions just as descriptive elements the formal elements of object words, or that evaluation 'is n icing on a cake of hard facts' (ibid., p. 25). It is quite another thi say, as Kovesi himself later seems to concede (ibid., pp. 56, 6 *passim*), that there are different purposes in forming moral and moral notions, surely one difference being that whereas non-n notions help us to classify the world, irrespective of our sentimer sympathies, moral notions are prescriptive or regulative accordi the way we evaluate actions, approvingly or disapprovi Beyond this it is of course still true that the *overall* purpo separating formal elements for purposes of their definability facilitate the formation of concepts for mutual communicatio arguability.
8. L. Wittgenstein, *Philosophical Investigations*, pp. 34, 43 (paras. 7
9. *Re Polemis* [1921] 3 K.B. 560. Though now overruled, the cas illustrates the point made in the text.
10. For the idea of 'defeasibility' see H. L. A. Hart, 'The Ascripti Responsibility and Rights', in A. Flew (ed.), *Logic and Lar* (Oxford: 1952) pp. 145, 148ff where however all norm concepts are regarded as equally defeasible, irrespective o distinction between intentional and non-intentional harm.
11. See, for example, D. Z. Phillips and H. O. Mounce, *Moral Pr* (London: 1970) p. 19ff.
12. J. L. Austin, *How to do Things with Words* (Oxford: 1962) pp. Indeed, as Austin further said, the commitment denoted promise' is 'stultified' by the denial of commitment in the p 'I ought not'. Or as Austin puts it a little later (ibid., p. 5 phrase 'I promise to do X but I am under no obligation to do it certainly look more like a self-contradiction – whatever tha than "I promise to do X, but I do not intend to do it"'.
13. H. A. Prichard, *Moral Obligation* (Oxford: 1949) p. 167ff.
14. Ibid., p. 177. Surprisingly Prichard maintains that there m something in this idea of an agreement after all. Because, thou express prior agreement seems clearly absurd, we have account for the fact that we do have the thought that by n certain noises we render ourselves bound to do a certain actio even though clear that we cannot have this thought on the ba prior express agreement, there must have been some such agre nevertheless, 'though from the nature of the case we must hav

Jurisprudence (Oxford: 1973) pp. 171, 183, 190ff.

14. Two other criticisms of the benefit theory (cf. Hart, op. cit., p. 192ff) seem in fact to strengthen that theory rather than to weaken it. (1) One criticism is that the benefit theory obscures the nature of *relative* duties, those in civil or private law over which the right-holder has exclusive control, rights therefore he can waive or give up, whereas as regards *absolute* duties, as those in criminal law, the victim has no such 'rights'. But, surely, even a victim of a crime may sometimes choose not to prosecute. And even if we do accept that a right-holder possesses a special privilege of control, this still does not affect the benefit theory, since what the right-holder can give up is only the benefit the duty-holder owes to him. Even where, as in criminal law, the right-holder cannot waive or give up anything, this is rather like the infant's inability to make agreements to give up (settle or compromise) civil rights. Thus the criminal right-holder, like the infant, now seems doubly protected; the benefit inhering in these rights is made even more secure. (2) Another criticism relates to a somewhat special topic, i.e. contracts for the benefit of third parties, as regards which the well-known common law rule is that the third party cannot enforce the contract not being an actual party to it, however much it is for his benefit. Here, argues Hart, the notion that a person must be a beneficiary is not even a necessary condition of having a right; for the intended beneficiary (the third party) has no contractual rights whereas the actual contracting party has, even though he is not the person intended to benefit by the contract. But, again, this does not really destroy the benefit theory. For this theory does not assert that all intended beneficiaries have rights, it only asserts that those who do have rights must be beneficiaries in a significant sense of that word. Even the contracting party above, though admittedly not the intended beneficiary under the contract, enjoys some benefit, that of procuring an advantage for a third party; for unless we can attribute to him such a benefit (the desire to see another benefited), we cannot rationally explain his 'motive' for making such a third party contract and for paying the price for it.

15. Glanville Williams, 'The Concept of Liberty' in R. S. Summers (ed.), *Essays in Legal Philosophy* (Oxford: 1968) pp. 121, 138.

16. Ibid., p. 141.

Index